UNREWARDED COURAGE

Other books by Brian Best

The Curling Letters of the Zulu War
Sister Janet
Burma Railway Man
Fighting for the News
Reporting from the Front
Reporting the Second World War
The Victoria Crosses that saved the Empire
The Desert VCs
The Forgotten VCs
The Victoria Cross Wars
The Victoria Cross in 100 Objects

UNREWARDED COURAGE

ACTS OF VALOUR THAT WERE DENIED THE VICTORIA CROSS

Brian Best

FRONTLINE
BOOKS

Unrewarded Courage
Acts of Valour that were denied the Victoria Cross

This edition published in 2020 by Frontline Books,
an imprint of Pen & Sword Books Ltd,
47 Church Street, Barnsley, S. Yorkshire, S70 2AS

ISBN: 978 1 52677 246 6

CIP data records for this title are available from the British Library.

For more information on our books, please visit
www.frontline-books.com email info@frontline-books.com
or write to us at the above address.

Printed and bound by TJ International
Typeset in 10.5/12.5 by Palatino

Contents

Glossary

abattis	(*abatis*) a defence made of felled trees placed lengthwise over each other with the boughs pointing outwards
ADC	Aide-de-camp
ADS	Advanced Dressing Station
AIF	Australian Imperial Force
AIR	Airborne Interception Radar
assegai	an iron-tipped spear
BAAT	British Army Training Team
bilharzias	a chronic disease, endemic in parts of Africa and South America, caused by infestation with blood flukes
cantonment	a military garrison or camp
CB	Companion of the Bath
CGC	Conspicuous Gallantry Cross
CD	Coastal Defence
CGM	Conspicuous Gallantry Medal (replaced in 1993 by the CGC)
CMG	Companion of St Michael and St George
COPP	Combined Operations Pilotage Party
DCM	Distinguished Conduct Medal (replaced in 1993 by the CGC)
DFC	Distinguished Flying Cross
DMI	Director of Military Intelligence
donga	a dry gulley
DSC	Distinguished Service Cross
DSO	Distinguished Service Order
EIC	East India Company
FAMP	Frontier Armed and Mounted Police (South Africa)
FAP	First Aid Post
fellaheen	Middle Eastern or North African farmers or agricultural labourers
Gaika	European name for the Ngquika people, Xhosa monarchy
ghazi	Muslim fighter
GOC	General Officer Commanding

HEIC	Honourable East India Company
IED	Improvised Explosive Device
impi	Zulu warriors
KCB	Knight Commander/Order of the Bath
KSLI	King's Shropshire Light Infantry
kraal	a village of huts or livestock enclosure
kopje	a small hill in a generally flat area
kukris	a curved knife typically used by Gurkhas
laager	an encampment formed by a circle of wagons
LRDG	Long Range Desert Group
MASB	Motor Anti-Submarine Boat
MC	Military Cross
MGB	Motor Gun Boat
MID	Mentioned in Despatches
ML	Motor Launch
MM	Military Medal
MO	Medical Officer
MTB	Motor Torpedo Boat
nullah	a riverbed or ravine
PFLOAG	Popular Front for the Liberation of the Occupied Arabian Gulf
PIAT	Projector, Infantry, Anti-Tank gun
pushteen	an Afghan outer garment
RAMC	Royal Army Medical Corps
RAP	Regimental Aid Post
RCAF	Royal Canadian Air Force
RCNVR	Royal Canadian Navy Volunteer Reserve
RDF	Rapid Deployment Force
rezai	a mud fort
RFC	Royal Flying Corps
RNAS	Royal Naval Air Service
RNVR	Royal Naval Volunteer Reserve
RPG	Rocket Propelled Grenade
sanger	(or sangar) a small fortified position usually constructed of stones
SAS	Special Air Service
SBS	Special Boat Service
Scud	Subsonic Cruise Unarmed Decoy missile
sepoy	Indian soldier serving under British or other European orders
SOE	Special Operations Executive
sowar	a rider or cavalry soldier
SRS	Special Raiding Squadron
tulwar	a sword or sabre

Introduction

During the ill-fated war against Russia (1853–56), the idea of a democratic gallantry medal was raised by a trio of men: William Howard Russell, *The Times's* special correspondent; the Duke of Newcastle; and Captain George Scobell MP. Little did they suspect the tangled ramifications the award would entail over the next two centuries.

The concept of a medal that would reward men from the ranks as well as officers below those senior commanders seemed fairly clear cut: a humble medal based on the design of the Peninsular Cross, a *cross pattée*, but made of bronze instead of gold; an explanatory warrant drawn up by the pedantic Prince Albert; and an investiture overseen by Queen Victoria. It all appeared to be straightforward enough but a series of bumps in the process led to ten appendices altering the original warrant over the next fifty years.

Russell, the journalist, learned from conversations in the camps of the bravery and stoicism displayed by the British soldier. He wrote suggesting the Queen might create an order of merit or valour and that it should bear her name. Russell's reports almost certainly influenced the Bath MP, Captain George Scobell, to raise the question in the House of Commons on 19 December 1854, requesting the bestowal of an 'Order of Merit to every grade and individual'.

This suggestion was taken up by the Duke of Newcastle, the Secretary of State for War. He was to be severely castigated in his handling of the British involvement in the war against Russia and subsequently sacked. He did, however, support the idea of a new democratic award when he wrote on 20 January 1855 to Prince Albert:

> I hope I am not taking too great a liberty if I ask Your Royal Highness's opinion upon the other suggestion, the institution of a new decoration to be confined to the Army and Navy, but open to all ranks of either service. ...
>
> I confess it does not seem right or politic that such deeds of heroism as this war had produced should go unrewarded by any distinctive outward mark of honour because they are done by

Privates or by Officers below the rank of Major, and it is impossible to believe that HM troops fighting side by side with those of France do not draw an invidious contrast between the rewards bestowed upon themselves and their allies.

The Duke was referring to the French example of the Médaille Militaire, established in 1852, which rewarded distinction on the field of battle. In December 1854, Great Britain did follow suit with the introduction of the Distinguished Conduct Medal (DCM) for the Army and the Conspicuous Gallantry Medal (CGM) for the Royal Navy, which had been approved by Queen Victoria. This was awarded for bravery to those of the Army rank of sergeant and below, and for the Royal Navy, petty officer and below. For the lower-ranked officers, the most they could expect was a mention in despatches or brevet. The opening sentence of the original VC warrant made this clear.

It has long been considered that there exists no means of adequately rewarding the individual gallant services of officers of the lower grades in the Military Service as well as Non-Comd. Officers and soldiers in the Army and Warrant Officers and Seamen in the Navy.

The institution of the Victoria Cross in 1856 became the first democratic award for gallantry to all ranks below major (Army) and captain (Royal Navy) and raised the interest amongst the British population. Thanks to the agitation of the media and Parliament in overcoming the opposition of the military hierarchy, Britain finally introduced a gallantry award for all ranks. This followed the example of two of Europe's major military nations: France and Prussia.

In 1813, Kaiser William Frederick III of Prussia ordered a new medal named the Iron Cross to be struck to replace flashier awards. The Iron Cross was of a simple design made from a base metal with no intrinsic value, similar to the Victoria Cross. It proved to be a brilliant public relations stroke as it equally rewarded his soldiers, irrespective of their rank, and had the effect of further unifying his army in the war against Napoleon.

A similar award, but more decorative, was conceived by Napoleon in 1802 with the introduction of the Légion d'Honneur. This was freely distributed to soldiers, sailors and civilians alike; in the case of the latter, mainly for political reasons. Napoleon famously declared: 'It is with such baubles that men are led.' It was decades later that Britain saw the merit in such an award.

Once the concept of a new gallantry award took root, the royal couple actively embraced their role in its development. The Royal Navy, under the command of the Admiralty, was the largest in the world. Although Queen Victoria was closely associated with her navy, she had little to do with its running. With the Army, she saw two ways of cementing her will with the service: firstly, the new award named after her provided a close association with the military; secondly, with the 1856 appointment of her cousin George, the Duke of Cambridge, as Commander-in-Chief, British Army. He was deeply devoted to the old army and worked with the Queen to block any reform proposal. His army became a moribund institution and, for most of Queen Victoria's reign, it lagged behind those of France and Germany.

The design of the medal was altered and approved by the Queen. She suggested using the motto 'For Valour' rather than 'For the Brave' on the grounds that all her soldiers were brave. A copper sample was sent to the Queen for approval but she rejected the choice of metal as it 'would soon look like an old penny'. Instead, she suggested that bronze would be more attractive and that it should be coated with a greenish varnish to protect it.

Appropriately, the bronze used was supplied by the cannon captured from the Russians during the Crimean War and readily available at the Woolwich Arsenal. Hancocks, the jewellers who had been appointed to supply the new award, soon found that bronze was too hard and broke the steel dies. There was little option but to resort to the wasteful process of sand casting and typically, twelve VCs were produced at a time. The crude casting required the Cross to be finished by hand chasing and careful filing to bring out the detail, thus making the finished article handmade, with no two alike. Every completed Cross was unique in the same way that fingerprints are to each of us.

At the beginning of the First World War, the bronze from the Russian cannon had almost run out. An apocryphal story has it that a couple of fitters at the Woolwich Arsenal were told to go into the storeroom and cut the cascabels (the large ball-like projection at the breech end around which recoil ropes were secured) from a couple of Russian cannon. Unable to identify the Russian guns, the fitters cut the cascabels from the two nearest cannon, which turned out to be Chinese. These were possibly captured in 1840, during the First Opium War. Thanks to the investigation by John Glanfield, and published in the *Journal of the Victoria Cross Society* (March 2006), the metal from the first Russian cannon has been shown to differ significantly from that of the two later Chinese guns. Since the beginning of the First World War, all but a few VCs issued in 1944 are made from gunmetal from the Chinese cannon.

So much for origins of the Victoria Cross. Now there came the request for submissions from the regiments and ships that had served in the Crimean War. And that is where the bureaucrats' best-laid plans began to founder.

Chapter 1

The Selection

It was in September 1856 that Horse Guards and the Admiralty instructed the commanding officers of the regiments and ships that had just returned from the Crimea to submit recommendations of their men who displayed outstanding bravery during the war. To adjudicate the submissions, the two departments formed selection boards to consider the recommendations. Unfortunately, the instructions had not been clear enough so it was left to the commanding officers to use their interpretation as to whom they should nominate for the new award.

Some were anxious to have their regiments shown in the most favourable light. The 77th (East Middlesex) Regiment put forward thirty-eight names, of which six were approved and two were finally gazetted (Sergeant John Park and Private Alexander Wright). Other cases included: the 47th (The Lancashire) Regiment, with sixteen submitted and one approved (Private John McDermond); the 49th (Hertfordshire) Regiment, with nine submitted with one approved (Lieutenant John Conolly); and the 68th (Durham) Regiment with twelve submissions and two approved (Private John Byrne and Captain John de Courcy Hamilton). Seven regiments – the 41st (Welsh), 42nd (Highland), 50th (Queen's Own), 56th (West Essex), 62nd (Wiltshire), 71st (Highland) and 79th (Cameron), all of whom had been heavily involved in the major Crimean battles – did not respond to the request for recommendations. It was suspected that it was not due to the absence of heroics by the officers and men but the lack of interest by the commanders of these regiments whose task it was to investigate the names of men who had distinguished themselves in battle.

When the Victoria Cross was instituted, rules or warrants were implemented to prevent the award from being diluted by being over bestowed. The Charge of the Light Brigade was the earliest case where there had been so many examples of exceptional bravery against huge odds that the participating regiments were asked to vote for just one representative from each unit. Prince Albert wrote a memo as early as 22 January 1855, in which he made such a point.

> How is a distinction to be made, for instance, between the individual services of the 200 survivors of Lord Cardigan's Charge? If you reward them all it becomes merely a Medal for Balaclava, to which the Heavy Brigade and the 93rd have equal claims.

He then suggested:

> That in cases of general action it [the VC] be given in certain quantities to particular regiments, so many to the Officers, so many to the sergeants, so many to the men (of the last say 1 per Company) and that their distribution be left to a jury of the same rank as the person to be rewarded … The limitation of the Numbers to be given to a Regiment at one time enforces the necessity of a selection and diminishes the pain to those who cannot be included.

It was not until late 1856 to early 1857 that the commanding officers of those regiments who did not submit recommendations were asked again for their candidates for the Cross. In the case of the Light Brigade, just a single name per regiment was submitted. There is one strange omission from this gallantry list: the 8th Hussars apparently did not submit a candidate for the Victoria Cross. The reason for this could be the fact that the commanding officer, Lieutenant Colonel Frederick Shewell, died at his home while on sick leave on 1 October 1855. This was around the time that the regiments began submitting their lists of recommended recipients and perhaps, with a change of commanding officer, this was overlooked or given a low priority. In another case of an incoming commanding officer, Lieutenant Colonel William Denny of the 41st wrote:

> On assuming command of the 41st (Welsh) Regiment, I find the circular dated September 20th, 1856, relative to the institution of the 'Order of the Victoria Cross' has not been replied to.
> I have the honour to state that after making a strict enquiry, I do not find that there are any Officers, Non Commissioned Officers or Soldiers in the 41st Regiment who could be considered eligible to be recommended for the most distinguished decoration.

A commanding officer who declined to recommend any of his men was Lieutenant Colonel Richard Waddy of the 50th. In a separate letter he described his gallantry in defending the trenches before Sebastopol on the night of 20/21 December 1854 and put himself forward for the Victoria Cross. This was declined and he had to be satisfied with a letter commending his steadfastness in repulsing the enemy.

Colonel Henry Warre of the 57th (West Middlesex) submitted thirty-one names made up of twenty-two privates, three corporals, seven sergeants, one lieutenant, two captains, one major, one lieutenant colonel and one colonel – Warre himself. The Awards Committee at Horse Guards whittled down this excessive list to just one to receive the Victoria Cross – Private Charles McCorrie.

After the abortive assault on the Great Redan on 5 June 1855, the British returned to their trenches and continued to exchange artillery fire with the Russians. It was during one such exchange that Private McCorrie performed his act of outstanding gallantry. A Russian shell, with its fuse fizzing, landed in McCorrie's trench. All but McCorrie froze with terror. The only man to react was McCorrie, who scooped up the heavy shell, carried it to the parapet and dropped it outside, where it exploded with a great roar.

His name appeared amongst the first VC recipients in the *London Gazette* dated 24 February 1857. His citation was a masterclass in brevity:

> On the night of the 23rd June, 1855, he threw over the parapet a live shell, which had been thrown from the enemy's battery.

He was destined not to physically receive his award. Charles McCorrie died in hospital on 8 April 1857 in Malta, where the 57th (West Middlesex) was stationed. He was buried in an unmarked grave at Msida Bastion Cemetery on the outskirts of Valletta. Colonel Warre, fearful that the regiment would lose its Victoria Cross, wrote the very next day to the commanding officer, General Pennefather, suggesting McCorrie's award should go to another on the list of his recommendations. As McCorrie's Cross had already been announced, there was no question of the award being denied. His engraved Cross was still sent to General Pennefather at Malta in June for presentation. It is not certain whether it was presented to a next of kin or returned to the War Office for posting to McCorrie's nearest relative.

The substitute VC was awarded to Sergeant George Gardiner for two acts of composure and steadiness with which he controlled his men. His Victoria Cross was belatedly presented to him on 5 October 1858 at a parade in Aden, en route to India.

It is of interest that McCorrie's Cross was the first ever VC to be offered at auction at Sotheby, Wilkinson & Hodge, on 21 February 1879, but failed to find a buyer. It is known that it is presently held privately.

The commanding officer of the 55th (Border) Regiment, Lieutenant Colonel Henry Daubeney, submitted thirty-two names, including his own. He wrote six pages explaining why he should receive the VC and submitted a list of thirteen witnesses, all from his regiment. The affidavits from the twelve privates were all written in the same hand and the wording was practically identical. Literacy among the other ranks was very low and it was noticeable that the affidavits were written by Lieutenant Colonel Daubeney.

On 18 December 1857, Lieutenant William Richards wrote a letter commending Henry Daubeney's handling of the regiment at the Battle of the Alma.

> The 55th Regiment having been thrown into great disorder owing to the difficult nature of the ground over which they had to advance towards the Alma under heavy fire. After having crossed the river we found ourselves opposed by two strong battalions of Russian Infantry which advanced down the hill towards us with a cloud of skirmishers in their front who maintained a galling and well directed fire on us, rendering it extremely difficult to rally the Regiment effectively. I was carrying the Regimental colours and the men had commenced gathering around them, when we were being outflanked by the enemy on our left. Colonel Daubeney came up and hurried me to the front and more to the left and by great exertion he succeeded in rallying the men as they crossed the river and formed them in line fronting the enemy and the Regiment was Sectioned to complete order, though under fire, so quickly that we were able to advance and charge the enemy columns up the hill with the bayonet without they being able to take advantage of our temporary confusion. At which moment they broke and took flight without us having to come close quarters.

This was verified by a statement from Lieutenant John Granville Harkness, late of the 55th (Border) Regiment. He sent a note to Henry Daubeney in which he wrote:

> I have perfect recollection of the circumstances. Richards and I often used to laugh at over the way we were shoved about on that occasion and how you shouted at us for not knowing in which way you wanted us to go. In fact, but for you, I don't think we could have got right again.

General Sir John Pennefather and General de Lacy Evans both wrote commending Daubeney of his handling of his men, but neither actually recommended him for the Victoria Cross.

A year later, he was still writing to Horse Guards but it was all to no avail as his self-recommendation was rejected and two other men were selected to receive the award (Private Thomas Beach and Major Frederick Elton).

One man of the 55th who was strongly considered was Colour Sergeant Charles Walker. Born in Derby, Charles Walker was a skinner by trade and very strongly built. He enlisted into the 55th (Border) Regiment at Trowbridge in 1840 and the following year made the long voyage to take part in the First China War. In 1844, he was promoted to corporal but six months later was reduced to the ranks for leaving the barracks without permission. From 1846 to 1849, his regiment was stationed in Ireland and witnessed the terrible effects of the potato famine. He was again promoted to corporal and, in 1855, was made a colour sergeant.

He displayed two acts of outstanding valour, one of which was witnessed by Private Thomas Leyland. He submitted his report to Lieutenant Colonel Daubeney, who recommended Walker for the Victoria Cross:

> For distinguished gallantry at the Battle of Inkerman 5th November 1854, in recapturing one of our Field Guns which was being dragged away by some of the enemy – and which but for the gallant and determined conduct of Sergeant Walker would have been carried off by the Russians.

His second exploit is referred to in Alexander William Kingslake's *Invasion of the Crimea.*

> In the earlier moments of the audacious attack, the Colour Sergeant – Charles Walker, a man of great size and strength – had wielded the butt-end of his rifle with prodigious effect, and now, when English and Russian soldiers became so jammed together that none could make use of their weapons, the huge Colour Sergeant was still fiercely driving a rank through part of the closely compressed crowd; doing this more or less by the power of his mighty shoulders and arms, but also by dint of the blows he rained on right and left with his fists, and those which he maintained with his feet against the enemy's ankles and shins.

The acts, which involved just forty men of the 55th against a whole Russian battalion, were enough to stall their attack and cause confusion. One would have thought these acts would have been enough to warrant a Victoria Cross but the Board of Officers deliberated differently. It was Private Thomas Beach who was awarded the VC for defending a wounded senior officer until help arrived. It would seem that defending a wounded senior officer ranked higher than a man who disrupted an enemy attack.

Charles Walker was awarded the Distinguished Conduct Medal on 20 August 1856, with a £10 annuity. He was discharged in 1861 and appointed Yeoman of the Guard. In 1881, he left to take up employment at the Royal Army Clothing Depot and died in 1886.

Another soldier who deserved the Victoria Cross was Lieutenant Colonel James Thomas Mauleverer, who came from a long line of military ancestors. Born in 1816, he joined the 17th (Leicestershire) in 1836 and was posted to New South Wales. Soon after, the regiment was sent to take part in the First Afghan War. They were part of the Bombay Contingent that, on 23 July 1839, attacked the citadel at Ghazni. In fierce night-time fighting, the Afghan defenders were defeated. For such a remote battle, the Ghazni Medal was struck and was the second medal awarded to all ranks for a specific battle after the Waterloo Medal.

In 1844 he transferred to the 30th (Cambridgeshire) as a captain and was with the regiment when it was sent to Crimea. He fought at the Battle of the Alma and was promoted to lieutenant colonel on the death of his commanding officer. In the early misty morning of 5 November, 115,000 Russians climbed the slopes of Inkerman to attack the weak British flank. The British could only muster 16,000 troops, who took the brunt of the Russian assault.

Around 6.00 am, the Russians were spotted making a three-pronged attack. General Pennefather ordered Mauleverer to take 200 of his men to guard the Barrier, which crossed one of the main routes. Lining up his men behind the Barrier, Mauleverer realised that he was confronting two battalions of the Borodino Regiment. As the Russians came on, Mauleverer gave the order to open fire. Due to the misty dampness, the cartridges misfired, leaving the soldiers helpless to stop the advance.

Once more, Mauleverer ordered his men to lie down behind the Barrier and fix bayonets. He waited and then leapt on top of the wall, with sword upraised, and ordered his men forward. The following charge took the Russian battalions by surprise. In the melee, Mauleverer was gravely wounded. As the depleted wing was beginning to run out of steam, they were joined by another wing of the regiment and some French reinforcements. Kingslake wrote in his history of the Crimean War:

> The shreds of the enemy's company columns, thrown back in a heap of confusion upon the solid mass coming up in support, seemed to

bring it to instant ruin, for that last body also, though it can scarce have felt English steel, began to fall back in disorder; and … the slender line of the 30th, with a remaining strength of perhaps seven or eight score soldiers, was driving a broken throng from the head of the Quarry Ravine up the slopes of Shell Hill.

The impact of this gallant charge was very considerable, for although only two of the Borodino battalions had been directly attacked by the 30th, the other two battalions were so unnerved by the defeat of their comrades that they too retreated and played no further part in the battle. Mauleverer's men had routed over twelve times their own numbers.

Mauleverer, modestly ignoring his own part in the battle, recommended his adjutant, Lieutenant Mark Walker, for the Victoria Cross, which was something the recently promoted colonel deserved. Adhering to the new warrant, he accepted that as commanding officer, he was ineligible. Recovering from his wound, he led his men in an attack on the Redan the following June, where he was wounded again. Although he did not receive the Victoria Cross, his gallantry was recognised with the Order of the Bath, the Savoyard Medal for Military Valour, the Turkish Order of Medjidie and the French Legion d'Honneur.

Mauleverer also recommended Corporal Colcutt, who earlier went to collect a string of mules being loaded with ammunition. A Russian shell landed amongst the animals, killing some and stampeding the rest. The pack saddles were set alight, with the danger that the ammunition would ignite and explode causing more deaths. Colcutt ignored the danger and beat out the flames. He then volunteered to carry the ammunition forward himself despite the heavy Russian fire. Although Colcutt's name was submitted, he was not successful.

One of the many anomalies of the Victoria Cross was quickly shown when Lieutenant Colonel the Honourable Henry Percy of the Grenadier Guards was awarded the Victoria Cross when he found himself with the men of several regiments nearly surrounded by the Russians. Because he knew the ground, he managed to extricate them and led them to an ammunition dump where they could rearm. His action was observed by the Duke of Cambridge, soon to be the commander of the British Army, who expressed his approval to Percy.

The other case involved Lieutenant Colonel Collingwood Dickson, on Lord Raglan's staff, who did little more than assist in carrying powder kegs under fire during the siege of Sebastopol. Quite why they were both singled out for the gallantry award when other commanders performed as well, if not with greater gallantry, is not apparent.

Both men were in positions where they could be seen by superiors and later recommended for the VC. Despite the wording of the first warrant, their higher rank was overlooked purely because Percy had been spotted by the Queen's cousin and Dickson was a member of Raglan's staff.

Lord Panmure declared that awards should be limited to the Crimean campaign. This did not stop some applications for past campaigns and battles. There were letters claiming the Victoria Cross for the Peninsular War as well as service in the 1847 New Zealand campaign. Replying to a letter from Colonel Luke Smythe O'Connor, 1st West India Regiment, Lord Panmure wrote: 'the terms of the warrant constituting the VC do not include foreigners among those eligible for the decoration.'

This was in response to an appeal to the War Office recommending the award of the VC to French Captain of Marines, Ducrest de Villeneuve. He was reported as having fought with valour against Muslim rebels in Combo in July and August 1855. O'Connor's request was denied as the War Office did not want the Cross to become a diplomatic award granted to make allied officers happy.

Two men from the 63rd (West Suffolk), John Brophey and James Slack, also put their names forward. Both had served as sergeants during the Crimean War and both had since been promoted from the ranks to lieutenant and ensign. Both men received endorsements from officers, including Colonel Dabzell. Ensign James Slack was particularly hopeful of a recommendation as he saved the life of Colonel Dabzell. To their disappointment, both applications were rejected, with no reason given. It may have been that a promotion to commissioned officer was reward enough, although there was resentment about sergeants being elevated to the officers' mess.

The list of men chosen for the first investiture appeared in the *London Gazette* on 24 February 1857. It totalled eighty-five recipients but by the time the Queen presented the Victoria Cross in Hyde Park on 26 June that year, those present had dropped to sixty-two due to postings abroad. One of the missing was Private William Stanlack of the Coldstream Guards, who was barred from attending as he had been accused of theft. Although brave in battle, he was a liability in peacetime. In 1858 he was caught drunk and asleep on guard duty and in 1862 was imprisoned for assault. The Coldstream Guards, although proud of his VC, were pleased to discharge him in 1863. It is strange that he did not join the list of six men stripped of their Crosses for various misdemeanours.

Another soldier strongly recommended for the Victoria Cross was Private Patrick McGuire of the 33rd (Duke of Wellington) Regiment.

Born in Manchester in 1837, he enlisted in the Army in November 1853, at the age of 17 years 3 months. He took part in the Battle of the Alma and the Siege of Sebastopol. On 17 October, around the time the artillery started its bombardment of the port, McGuire was on picket duty when he was captured. The incident was recorded by Colonel the Honourable Somerset Gough Calthorpe on 23 October.

> You hear every day of heroic acts of bravery by the soldiers: one I call to mind. A few days ago a private of the 33rd (Duke of Wellington) Regiment was surprised and made prisoner by two Russian soldiers when on advanced Sentry. One of these worthies took possession of his musket and the other his pouch and marched him between them towards Sebastopol. The Englishman kept a wary watch and when he fancied his captors off their guard sprang on the one who had his musket, seized it and shot dead the other of his foes who carried the pouch as well as his own arms and accoutrements. Meanwhile the Russian from whom our fellow had taken his own musket and who had fallen to the ground, when rising from his recumbent position fired, missed and finally had his brains knocked out by the butt end of the Englishman's musket; after which the man coolly proceeded to take off the Russian accoutrements etc., with which he returned laden to his post where he had been surprised, fired at by the Russian sentries, and received with cheers by our own pickets.

McGuire's act was met with great approval. Lord Raglan immediately authorised a gratuity of £5 and, when the Distinguished Conduct Medal was instituted in December 1854, McGuire was one of the first to be decorated. He was also awarded the French Médaille Militaire. Back in England, three different prints depicting McGuire's exploit were produced and he briefly became a public hero.

When the commanding officers were asked to submit names for the Victoria Cross, Lieutenant Colonel John Johnson considered McGuire was worthy and recommended his name. In due course, the citation arrived before the Queen and, on 17 February 1857, she wrote to the Secretary of State for War, Lord Panmure, objecting to McGuire's name.

> There is only one case which the Queen thinks had better be omitted, viz Private P. McGuire of the 33rd. His deed, although publicly praised and rewarded by Lord Raglan, was one of very doubtful morality, and if pointed out by the Sovereign as praiseworthy, may lead to the cruel and inhumane practice of never making prisoners, but always putting to death those who may be overpowered for fear of their rising over their captors.

Victoria's reasoning is baffling and it shows that Prince Albert's philosophical influence was probably involved. Lord Panmure concurred and Patrick McGuire's name was removed from the list, thus making the 33rd the only regiment not to receive a Victoria Cross during the Crimean War.

McGuire continued to serve with the 33rd but in 1861, he was medically discharged suffering from 'enlargement of the liver and spleen from dyspepsia … His ailments have not been aggravated by vice and misconduct.' He died less than a year later at his home in Manchester.

There were cases of men who considered that they had done enough to claim the Victoria Cross. Unable to obtain his commanding officer's consent to forward an application, Private Robert Thimbley of the 44th (East Essex) Regiment began a succession of letters to the Duke of Cambridge claiming that he was entitled to the new award. He sent a claim together with a statement made by Lieutenant Colonel Clement Alexander Edwards of the 18th (Royal Irish) Regiment, who had observed his conduct during the abortive assault on the Redan on 18 June 1855.

> In the attack that took place yesterday by the 2nd Brigade 3rd Division we especially remarked the conduct of Private Robert Thimbley 44th Regiment who distinguished himself by his gallant conduct while in the most advanced spot. We also know that he attended to the wounded of the several Regiments engaged under a most heavy fire.
>
> His soldierlike behaviour and assistance rendered to the officers during the occupation of the advanced Houses were particularly remarked. He also volunteered for and was one of the advance guard.

The Duke set in motion an enquiry as to Thimbley's claim. Colonel Charles Staveley of the 44th had not witnessed any of Thimbley's action and concluded his statement with: 'There is not a man in the Regiment who considers that he is entitled to the decoration he claims.'

Further examination of Thimbley's service record reveals that he was batman to two officers and spent little time, except for three or four days in June, in the trenches. He was then sent to help build a hut for General Sir William Eyre but was dismissed from the work party under strong suspicion of theft. One would have thought that he would have given up his claim. Instead, he continued to write to the Duke until February 1869 and received yet another rejection. At this point he must have given up or was deceased.

Thimbley's persistence pales in comparison with the deluge of correspondence sent by one of the Light Brigade Chargers – Thomas Morley. Morley was a Nottingham-born corporal in the 17th Lancers whose military service record rivals that of George MacDonald Fraser's 'Harry Flashman'. Resentful that he was not in line to receive the Victoria Cross or even the Distinguished Conduct Medal, he began a forty-year campaign to have his gallantry recognised. For an 'other ranker' he was good at expressing himself in the actions he either took part in or made up. Disappointed and angry that he had been overlooked for the new award, he left the Army in 1857 and began his torrent of correspondence. Morley's first attempt to secure the award was made to the editor of *The Times* on 24 April 1857.

> I am a sergeant of nearly three years, lately retired from the 17th Lancers, at the early age of 25 years, solely in consequence of being passed over most unjustly in the rewards and honours that have been bestowed. I am now made drill sergeant in the Sherwood Rangers, Mansfield, by its noble colonel His Grace the Duke of Newcastle, and, wishing my fellow men to know how unjustly I have been treated, I beg of you to allow me a place in your columns, so generously open to private as well as public grievances, to state my service as briefly as possible. After being at Alma, I was present with my regiment in every engagement that took place.
>
> I charged at Balaclava with my squadron until it was nearly annihilated, my own lance being shot away. Drawing my sword I galloped on to the Russian guns, and assisted in cutting down the gunners. On the right of our forming line I observed one particular gun going away as fast as the horses could take it. I went after it with Captain Jervis, of the 13th Light Dragoons, who shot one of the horses and delayed its progress. On this I engaged two of the gunners, who both fell.
>
> It now became a struggle for our lives; a large body of Cossacks surrounded us. I succeeded in working my way through them, and galloped in the direction of what I judged to be our own Hussars. I found they were Russians reforming. I forced my way on full speed through them, unhurt. A regiment of Polish Lancers, 800 strong, had formed across the valley. I halted a moment to look around. Perceiving several of our cavalry in the same dilemma, I called to them, and being then a corporal, I used what authority I had to form them as well as I could. We gathered 12 and charged their centre; most of us got through. I believe three fell. These men were 4th and 13th Light Dragoons and 17th Lancers; one was of the 8th Hussars. I received the point of a lance in the right hand; the wound was slight.

Private James Wightman was one of several cavalrymen who heard Morley's Midlands voice call out: 'Coom 'ere, coom 'ere, fall in, lads fall in!' The dozen or so troopers gathered to him and charged through the Polish Lancers as if they were not there. Morley continued with his bitter plea for an award.

> I was present at every skirmish in which my regiment was engaged and I returned home when the campaign ended. When I was in Ireland I inquired of my troop officer why I did not get a medal for distinguished conduct. He told me he was very sorry I did not, but it lay to the commanding officer's discretion. So it appears they are not 'distinguished conduct medals' but 'discretion medals'!
>
> There are several men in the 17th Lancers who wear medals for distinguished conduct on the field of battle who never crossed swords with a Russian. This is my simple and truthful statement and I think I have reason to complain that I am not decorated with a cross of valour – not to wear as a matter of vanity, but alone prizable to me as a mark that, though young, I have not been an unworthy soldier.

On 17 July, his second target was Lord Panmure, who instructed the Whitehall servants to reply that all claims should be made through HRH the General Commander-in-Chief. There followed decades of claims and rejections.

Thomas Morley knew little except soldiering. He was not just addicted to war; he was also addicted to the idea that he was a great man. With the outbreak of the Civil War in the United States, he travelled there and volunteered for the Union Army. On 25 July 1862, he joined a mounted regiment, the 12th Pennsylvania Cavalry, and was appointed second lieutenant. Within two months he was captured when his horse was killed and he was briefly imprisoned at Richmond, Virginia. It is thought he was taken prisoner during the Battle of Manassas or First Bull Run, and was part of a prisoner exchange. He used this incident to apply for the Medal of Honour, stating:

> Unfortunately for myself, my horse was shot and I was taken prisoner together with Lieutenant McCalier and John H. Black. This was the first time General 'Stonewall' Jackson was ever defeated by a Federal Officer and such conspicuous service in action I think you will clearly agree distinguished one for gallantry and intrepidity above my comrades. I need no particular individual to voice the matter for me. The whole Regiment knows what I did and they are facts that will live in history. Again it must not be forgotten that against tremendous odds I laid down my life as a sacred duty to save my Regiment and the country owe me this honourable distinction and thanks further to Major Egerton Jerry will tell you if asked. I was the only Officer who knew Military tactics in the Regiment and what the 12th Pennsylvania Cavalry knew they owed to my

energy and experience. Such testimony needs no words of mine to prove to you what was thought of me in the Regiment.

Morley rather over-egged his account by saying the great Confederate general, 'Stonewall' Jackson, had been embarrassed by Morley's action. The fact was that the Union Army was soundly beaten and retreated back to Washington. This was another example of Morley lobbying for a gallantry award. His Civil War service included another capture and imprisonment, this time in the notorious Libby Prison in Richmond. He ended his service as a captain at the end of the Civil War and returned to England.

He took up the post of troop sergeant major with the Ayrshire Yeomanry and lived in Robbie Burns's cottage. Over the nineteenth century, many families had lived in Burns Cottage, running the dwelling as a public house. Thomas Morley and his family were the last people to reside there. He also attended the First Balaclava Banquet in 1875 but, in 1884, returned to the United States.

For nine years he was employed as a clerk in the War Department in Washington. He worked in a building that had at one time been the Ford Theatre, where Abraham Lincoln was assassinated, and in 1866 it had been taken over by the War Department as a store and offices. On 9 June 1893, the front collapsed, bringing down two stories and killing twenty-two workers and injuring sixty-eight others. One of the injured included Morley. He was unable to work but continued to write to Horse Guards, claiming the Victoria Cross and blackening the names of some of his fellow soldiers. One letter he wrote on 12 November 1896 from his home in Washington was to the new Commander-in-Chief, British Army, Field Marshal Lord Wolseley. Morley filed two sworn statements in which he attributes his failure to secure a Victoria Cross to the newly promoted 17th Lancers' commanding officer, Colonel Henry Roxby Benson. He wrote:

> Colonel Benson was allowed to turn Her Majesty's and Princes Consort Noble Order and the Royal Warrant into a mockery and the Victoria Cross into a sham. He was the cause of me receiving an official letter dated 8th October 1857, stating that all claims for the Victoria Cross must be founded upon facts. This Colonel Benson wrote the most cruel false statements to the Commander-in-Chief, and was the cause of me purchasing my discharge out of the 17th Lancers, and then losing promotion in the Yeomanry. He made false statements respecting my being promoted top sergeant. I can prove I was promoted in November 1854. I have received all kinds of official letters telling me they see no reason to open my case.

I received an official letter dated 22nd February 1892, stating that the case cannot now be opened.

Morley continued his diatribe against Colonel Benson, accusing him of flogging some of the men who took part in the Balaclava Charge. He also singled out Sergeant Charles Wooden, later promoted to regimental sergeant major, for special invective.

Colonel Benson had a Regimental Sergeant Major Wooden, a foreigner, that could not speak the English language when he joined the regiment, went by the name of 'Tish-me'. Colonel Benson went by the name of 'Dosey', he always looked as if he was asleep. But when he played cards with young officers they found out he was not dreaming. Colonel Benson and this Wooden, their teeth fit in their jaws like hyenas. Every officer and soldier feared them.

Thomas Morley was now in his seventies and his constant search for a Victoria Cross was running out of steam. One last throw came with the publication of his booklet about his Crimean experiences entitled *The Cause of the Charge of the Light Brigade*, published in 1899. He lived with his family in Nottingham, where he died on 14 August 1906.

The mention of Sergeant Charles Wooden brings up the rejection of Bosun's Mate James Doran. Born in 1818 at Workington, Cumberland, he joined the Royal Navy in 1836 aboard HMS *Carysfort*. From 1843 to 1847, he served with Her Majesty's Coastguard before rejoining the Navy. He advanced to petty officer 1st class and joined HMS *Agamemnon* as bosun's mate and remained in her for the duration of the Crimean War.

He was strongly recommended for the Victoria Cross by Admiral Lord Lyons, who witnessed Doran's outstanding gallantry. During the Fleet bombardment of Sebastapol and Fort Constantine, a shell landed on Lord Lyons' flagship, *Agamemnon*, and started a fire. Lyons wrote a VC recommendation, dated 10 May 1856, for all four men who fought the blaze, in which he stated:

When the Mainsail of the *Agamemnon* was set on fire during the general Action of the 17 Oct 1854, Mr Spilsbury, Charles Willis, William Allen and James Doran immediately ran aloft and remained in the Main Yard under very heavy fire until they had succeeded in extinguishing the fire – during that time the Mainmast head and Main Yard were struck several times.

James Doran must have been made of heroic stuff for he was earlier awarded a silver Royal Humane Society medal. In January 1843, he plunged into a storm-ravaged sea in an attempt to rescue a shipmate who had been swept overboard and could not swim. Doran was successful in bringing the man alongside but he was already dead.

Eleven men received the new Conspicuous Gallantry Medal. Doran had already applied for the Victoria Cross and Admiral Lord Lyons had endorsed Doran's application. The claim went forward and arrived at the Admiralty on 11 January 1857. As with much of Whitehall bureaucracy, the application moved slowly through the various departments. As a consequence, it missed the list of applications set before the Queen on 15 February and so was not included in the *London Gazette* on 24 February 1857. A member of the Admiralty Board made the decision about Doran's submission with the tart comment: 'Too late for grant of Victoria Cross – [Doran] to be awarded the Conspicuous Gallantry Medal and gratuity of £15 …'

In fact, further Crimean War VC citations appeared in the *London Gazette* on 5 May, 23 June, 25 September and 20 November 1857, 2 June and 26 October 1858 and 6 May 1859.

This made a mockery of the application by Charles Wooden, who claimed a Victoria Cross as he had accompanied Surgeon James Mouat in rescuing Captain Morris, who had lain wounded on the battlefield. Mouat was awarded the VC but Wooden, who was then serving in India, was not. Despite the lateness of the claim, he was gazetted on 26 October 1858, nearly two years after Doran's application.

Even later than Wooden's tardy application came a letter from Major Frederick Miller of the Royal Artillery. He wrote that he had performed a similar act at the Battle of Inkerman, for which another officer had been rewarded with the Victoria Cross. The Awards Committee apologised, saying that the application had been mislaid and that Miller's citation would be gazetted on 6 May 1859. Although this was the final Crimean VC, two further applicants lobbied for the award to no avail: Barrack Sergeant Bacon and Private James Aitken.

There seems to have been confusion regarding the exploits rewarded by the Victoria Cross (1857) and both the Distinguished Conduct Medal for the Army (1854) and the Conspicuous Gallantry Medal (1855) for the Royal Navy. The fact that all three gallantry awards were instituted within three years of each other muddied the water regarding who was eligible for the top award for gallantry.

Some non-commissioned officers and other ranks who received the DCM during the Crimean War also received the Victoria Cross for the same act. These were Thomas Grady, William Stanlack, John Byrne, George Gardiner, William Coffey and Alfred Ablett. Those naval personnel who received the Victoria Cross also received the

Conspicuous Gallantry Medal. These were John Sullivan, Joseph Trewavas, George Ingouville, William Rickard and John Taylor. The latter died on the day the first VC citations appeared in the 24 February 1857 edition of the *London Gazette*. Although these men were told not to wear their DCMs and CGMs, they all displayed them across their chests. Such are the vagaries of the rules of the Victoria Cross.

Chapter 2

Indian Problems

The Persian War

Wedged in-between the Crimean War and the Indian Mutiny was the Anglo-Persian War, fought from 1 November 1856 until 4 April 1857. Although it eventually produced three VCs, all East India Company officers, it rejected a strong claim for another, James Rennie, of the Indian Navy. He was born in 1814 and at the age of 13 joined the Indian Navy. During the First China War of 1842, he was in command of the Honourable East India Company (HEIC) ship *Sesostris* covering the landings of the troops and Royal Marines under intense fire from the fortresses and batteries. He also commanded his marines against the defences at Tinghae, Chinhae, Ningpo Tsekee, Chapoo and Nanking.

With the First Burma War of 1852, Rennie was promoted to commander of *Zenobia* and led his blue jackets into the jungle, where he trapped a Burmese army of 3,000. For this example of 'gun-boat diplomacy', Rennie was presented with the Sword of Honour from the East India Company.

Taking part in the Persian campaign, Rennie was given command of the HEIC ship *Firoze*. He was ordered by General Sir James Outram to attack Mohammerah, a fortress at the head of the Persian Gulf. Outram wrote in his report:

> On 24 March, a boat with muffled oars proceeded up the river to choose a position for a mortar battery, but when closely under the forts, it was discovered that the selected site for the mortar was a swamp. The ingenuity of Commander Rennie came to the rescue with proposal of a mortar raft and in defiance of the engineers who said the first shot would smash it, a raft was constructed during the night, under Commander Rennie's direction, of casks and studding sail booms securely lashed together and being manned by the Bombay Artillery … the Indian Navy frigates proceeded

to the attack. The *Firoze* and *Assaye* then moved to within sixty yards of the earthworks and at about 10 o'clock the magazine of the northern fort blew up. ... The British loss was only ten killed and thirty wounded. The Persian Army of 13,000 was beaten and dispersed losing some 300 killed.

It was further reported that:

Commander Rennie's happy thought of placing around the bulwarks of several vessels trusses of pressed hay in which the musket balls of the Persian matchlock men lodged without injury to anyone, thus 300 bullets were found buried in the sides of the *Firoze* and vast numbers were taken out of the hay trusses.

Some, I hope, may gain even the greatest of all distinctions, the Victoria Cross. One especially, Commander Rennie of the Indian Nay, will be found to have earned a just claim to it.

Eventually, Outram's recommendation reached the Admiralty, who turned it down on:

the grounds that his acts in taking a mortar battery on a raft under the Persian batteries, taking a boat through fire in order to accelerate the advance of the troops, and leading an expedition which destroyed stores in the face of a large enemy army on the opposite bank of a river, had all been acts of duty.

Despite the disappointment of not receiving the Victoria Cross, Rennie took comfort in being awarded the Companion of the Bath (CB).

On 23 May 1857, General Outram wrote to the chairman of the HEIC stating that he would submit the names of individual officers who were worthy of distinction. Among them was Captain John Worgan, Bombay Artillery, who put two 8-inch and two 5½-inch mortars on Rennie's raft. The following night he was towed by the steamship *Comet* to a sheltered spot behind an island, where he moored. At daybreak the mortars began lobbing shells into Muhammerah Fort. At the same time, the Navy sailed up and began pounding from the front. Once more, the infantry bayonets were to be deprived of blood for under this unexpected attack the Persian Army withdrew, abandoning tents, guns and equipment. Worgan was recommended for the VC but this was not approved.

General Outram, who was notoriously generous with his awards, had recommended ten of the 3rd Bombay Cavalry for the Victoria Cross. This occasion was a rare event when about 240 cavalry charged and broke a 700-strong Persian square at Khushab. It was conventional wisdom that it was impossible for cavalry to penetrate a square of steady infantry, although in 1846, the 16th Lancers managed this against the Sikhs at Aliwal.

Under the command of Captain John Forbes, the 240 sabres did not hesitate to crash through the facing side of the square. As he forced his way in, Forbes was shot in the hip and was severely wounded. As Lieutenant Moore leapt into the middle of the enemy, his horse was shot beneath him and he fell heavily to the ground. In his fall his sword broke in half and he staggered up, defending himself as best he could. His friend, John Malcolmson, seeing the imminent danger he was in, forced his way through the enemy, gave Moore a stirrup and then brought him through the fighting to safety. Both were later awarded the Victoria Cross.

In 1860, Forbes wrote to apply for the new gallantry medal but received a reply from the Duke of Cambridge, pointing out that, although he had shown great gallantry in leading his regiment into the square, his application had been turned down. Instead, he was promoted to major and awarded the Companion of the Bath. He was specially recommended to 'the favourable notice of the Government for meritorious service'.

The three VCs awarded for the briefly fought war against Persia include two to the 3rd Bombay Light Cavalry. Captain John Wood of 20th Bombay Native Infantry had written wistfully in his diary, dated 27 March 1857, soon after his gallant act on 9 December 1856 at Bushire:

> That is, that they (the 64th Staffordshire) came in as soon as me and my company, however that the attempt deprived us of our right was ever made was owing to my immediate superiors not having pushed my claim. It is a bitter pill to find one's self ever crushed, and every attempt made to depreciate one – but I must remember last Sunday's text, 'Fret not thyself!' I feel I ought to feel thankful that my life was spared, that, although I received eight wounds, not one was fatal. Everyone says that I ought to get the Victoria Cross, but no one applies for it for me.

A new warrant was drawn up recognising the gallantry of white members of the HEIC during the Indian Mutiny. As an afterthought, the three officers in the Persian War were also recommended to receive the Victoria Cross. They had to wait nearly four years, until: 9 November 1860 (Lieutenant John Malcolmson, 3rd Bombay Light Cavalry); January 1861 (Captain John Wood, 20th Bombay Native Infantry); and 18 October 1861 (Lieutenant Arthur Moore, 3rd Bombay Light Cavalry).

Indian Mutiny

There has perhaps been no event in the history of India that has captivated historians and ordinary readers as the variously named Indian Mutiny, the Sepoy Rebellion or the First Indian War of

Independence. The outbreak of the Indian Mutiny at Meerut on 10 May 1857 saw the white officers of the Honourable East India Company confronted with the long-held rage of their Bengali sepoys. Captain Martineau, a senior musketry instructor at Ambala, was approached by the NCOs of the Native Infantry pleading their case. Martineau wrote to the Assistant Adjutant General at the end of April 1857, warning: 'The state of affairs is lamentable as it discloses the actual feelings of the whole of the Native Army. … They (sepoys) placed in my hands letters from various regiments which convinced me a widespread conspiracy was matured.'

Within days, the Meerut mutiny heralded the start of the uprising, which spread throughout Oude, Rohilkhand and some neighbouring states. The Indian Mutiny produced a number of 'firsts', including: the most VCs won on a single day – twenty-four at the Second Relief of Lucknow on 16 November 1857; the VC brothers, Charles and Hugh Gough; the oldest VC, 63-year-old William Raynor; Thomas Flinn, who, at the age of 15 years 3 months, was acknowledged as one of the two youngest VCs; the ballot was used for the first time; of the forty-six awarded in this way, twenty-nine relate to the Mutiny; and, for the first time, there was a recommendation for a second VC bar. It also saw the changes to the warrant. Three appendices were introduced during the Indian Mutiny, one of which was not welcomed by the Whitehall civil servants.

On 29 October 1857, Appendix V of the warrant extended eligibility to white soldiers of the Honourable East India Company. For the first time since its inception, the VC was awarded to soldiers not under the direct control of the Crown. The fathers from less well-to-do families put their sons through Addiscombe College to enter the HEIC military establishment. The alternative was to pay an exorbitant sum to join one of Her Majesty's regiments.

Lieutenant William Alexander Kerr of the 24th Bombay Native Infantry was one of the first HEIC officers to be recommended for the Victoria Cross, which was initially turned down mainly through prejudice against non-Imperial servicemen on the part of the War Office. It was accepted after an appeal and published in the *London Gazette* on 24 April 1858.

> On the breaking out of the mutiny in the 27th Bombay Native Infantry in July 1857, a party of mutineers took up a position in the stronghold, or *paga*, near the town of Kolapore, and defended themselves to extremity. Lieutenant Kerr, of the Southern Mahratta Irregular Horse, took a prominent share of the attack on the position,

and at the moment when its capture was of great public importance, he made a dash at one of the gateways, with some dismounted horsemen, and forced an entrance by breaking down the gate. The attack was completely successful, and the defenders were either killed, wounded or captured, a result that may with perfect justice be attributed to Lieutenant Kerr's dashing and devoted bravery.

(Letter from the Political Superintendent at Lolapore to the Adjutant-General of the Army dated 10 September 1857.)

Five East India Company officers were put forward by the Indian Government for the Victoria Cross. In a memo dated March 1863, their names were noted in the margin. Edward Pennington wrote:

Of these, Sir Charles Wood rejected Major McGowan, Bombay Army, Lieutenant Clifford Meacham and Lieutenant Martin of the Bengal Army that they had failed to establish their claims and His Royal Highness has hesitated to recommend the two others to the Secretary of State, although submitting Sir Charles Wood's recommendation in their favour. Their cases were therefore rejected.

The most senior of the five was Lieutenant Colonel James Macleod Bannatyne Fraser-Tytler. He was acting as Assistant Quartermaster General with Sir Henry Havelock's column as they attempted the First Relief of Lucknow. Fraser-Tytler was present in all twelve actions during the relief, having his horse shot under him and was dangerously wounded in the advance through the narrow streets. His share in the day's events is related in a letter written by Lieutenant Harry Havelock, who experienced a similar action a few weeks before at Cawnpore. Having overcome resistance outside Lucknow, they faced the guns on the Char-Bagh Bridge.

In this situation Lieutenant Colonel Fraser-Tytler rode up and immediately proceeded to reconnoitre the position under a most heavy fire. Forming an opinion that the bridge could be carried with a bayonet charge, while (as the enemy's artillery fire was superior) further delay would not only be useless but dispirit the troops, he represented his views to Brigadier-General Neill and prevailed on that officer that the attempt should be made. On receiving permission he carried the orders to advance to the 1st Madras Fusiliers and assisted in collecting the men who had been dispersed under cover in some huts for shelter.

Lieutenant Colonel Fraser-Tytler rode with the leading section, but as it came on the bridge-head, the enemy fired its last round of grape, by which his horse was struck down. Before he could disengage, the bridge was carried. Immediately afterwards the enemy opened fire from two concealed guns which covered the bridge, which was in our position, in reverse. Lieutenant Colonel Fraser-Tytler immediately ascertained the position of these guns and reported to General Havelock on the advisability of them being captured by the infantry, as from their situation, no artillery could be brought to bear on them and their fire was fearful with telling effect on the rear of our column with the train of baggage crowded in a narrow road between walls.

He was directed by the General to order the nearest regiment to take the guns and he guided the 90th Light Infantry to the spot. The regiment carried the two pieces with a rapid charge. Lieutenant Colonel Fraser-Tytler directed throughout on foot, holding by the mane of Colonel Campbell's horse during the attack.

General Outram praised Fraser-Tytler's action and General Napier stated, 'I am sure if Havelock's whole force had the power of conferring the Victoria Cross for general conduct and devoted gallantry, they would confer it on Lieutenant Colonel Fraser-Tytler.'

The only other candidate identified from the five signatures is that of Lieutenant Clifford Henry Meacham of the 7th Oudh Irregular Infantry. He took part in the abortive Battle of Chinhut before retreating to the Residency in Lucknow. On 18 August 1857, he was on lookout on a building in Sikh Square on the perimeter of the Residency's defensive barricade. He later wrote:

It was here that Captain Orr and myself with ten Christian drummers who formed part of the garrison, were blown into the air by the explosion of a mine. I can assure my readers that an involuntary ascent of some twenty or thirty feet into the air in the form of a spread eagle is by no means an agreeable sensation; and I was very thankful when I kissed mother earth again, albeit I should have considered it rather too warm a maternal embrace on any other occasion.

The explosion tore a 30-foot hole in the outer wall of the second enclosure and a general call prevented the mutineers from getting inside the Residency. When Meacham and his co-defenders were finally relieved in November 1857, he joined Hodson's Horse. On 13 June 1858, at Nawabgunge, Henry Daly, who had taken over Hodson's Horse, wrote:

The ground between us and the enemy on the right is well adapted for cavalry, for, although there was a ravine within a few yards of their front, it was sufficient to stop a horse; as I deployed to make the charge. I detached Lieut. Meacham with Lieut. The Hon.

J.H. Fraser and one hundred sabres to cross the ravine and to bear down on their left flank. Finding the enemy in greater strength than could be observed from the front, this officer judiciously delayed the movement till the advance on the left hook took place. I must regret the state that in gallantly making the charge over broken ground, Lieutenant Meacham was severely wounded, his horse received a couple of bullets and two sword cuts.

Clifford Meacham was subsequently mentioned in General Hope Grant's report and was in line for the Victoria Cross. Having submitted their recommendation for the Victoria Cross, along with their three other comrades, Fraser-Tytler and Meacham were refused.

General Sir Colin Campbell was one of the old school, who did not approve of the Victoria Cross. He was constantly sidetracked by officers claiming the new award so he invoked Clause 13 of the warrant, which directed each regiment to elect four recipients: one officer, one NCO and two privates. This offhand manner only provoked further dissent, with one officer complaining that a quartermaster sergeant got the medal because he doled out the grog. The 9th Lancers, who had hardly engaged the enemy, submitted their native *bheesti* (water carrier), while another officer accused Campbell of trying 'to lower and degrade the order'. This system used in the Indian Mutiny rather inflated the number of VCs awarded, with twenty-nine recipients receiving their Crosses by ballot.

The rules governing the awarding of the Victoria Cross were added to and amended during the conflict and Queen Victoria signed three royal warrants in 1857–58. Kerr received his VC on 4 December 1858 from Major General F.T. Farrell at Belgaum, India. Many of the Indian Army VCs soon followed suit.

In November 1857, General Campbell's column approached Lucknow with the intention of relieving the Residency. Instead of following the previous attempt, which had run the gauntlet of narrow streets and ambush points, they were guided by two civilian messengers: Thomas Kavanagh and Kunoujee Lal. Advised to keep clear of the city, the column skirted to the south-east and north of Lucknow and approached the Residency via an area of palaces and gardens.

It was widely known that Sir Colin favoured his old regiment, the 93rd Highlanders, who amassed a record number of Victoria Crosses during the raising of the siege of the Residency. In the glorious charge to take the Secundra Bagh, the 93rd took no prisoners and killed some 2,000 sepoys and rebels within its walls. Led by Lieutenant Colonel

John Ewart, they searched for and despatched those who hid in the gloom of the palace.

In one dark room, two mutineers stood to defend their colours. Ewart rushed in to capture the flags and was hacked twice with the *tulwars* (swords). Ignoring the wounds, Ewart killed both rebels and grabbed one of the colours. By this time the fighting had died down and Ewart went in search of Sir Colin. When he found him he was dismayed at the reception he received: 'Damn you, sir! What business have you to be taking flags? Go back to your men!'

Sir Colin later apologised to Ewart. The 93rd voted Ewart for the Victoria Cross, but Campbell refused to submit a recommendation.

On 17 November, Captain Garnet Wolseley of the 90th Light Infantry was ordered by Colin Campbell to storm the Mess House of the 32nd Regiment, formerly the Khoorsheyd Munzil Palace. A fellow officer who was with Wolseley confirmed that the General had promised Wolseley the Victoria Cross if he fulfilled this order. During the Crimean War, Wolseley had also been recommended for the Victoria Cross by Sir William Gordon, Commander of the Royal Engineers at Sebastopol. He had displayed outstanding gallantry during the 7 June 1855 attack on the Redan. Gordon was also present when Wolseley lost an eye during an exchange of fire on 30 August.

With Captain William Peel's Naval Brigade firing at the thick walls, Wolseley, followed by his men, ran across open ground to the garden wall. Clambering over, he found several matchlock men who fired at him. Sprinting across the drawbridge, he called to his bugler to sound the advance. He then ran up the steps to the roof and planted the Union flag, inviting a flurry of shot from the rebels. Thomas Kavanagh wrote in his book *How I Won the Victoria Cross*, 'Captain Wolseley, who delighted in dash and danger, fell upon the enemy as they tried to escape, and in half an hour he was seen on top of the inner building, waving the British banner.'

It was now mid-afternoon and the progress of the 90th and some Sikhs was observed by Martin Gubbins and General Havelock in the Residency. They also saw Captain Wolseley raise the Union flag on the right-hand tower of the Mess House and knew that relief was close at hand.

Realising that they had taken their objective fairly easily, Wolseley then led his company to attack the Motee Mahul some 300 yards distant. The gateway was blocked by rocks and masonry and a few men attempted to dislodge the barrier with crowbars and pickaxes. Private Andrews, who had been Wolseley's servant in Crimea, ran out to lead his comrades forward but was met with shots from the loopholes. Wolseley immediately sprinted to Andrews, picked him up and staggered back to safety. Unfortunately, another shot hit and further wounded Andrews, who nevertheless survived into old age. A hole had been knocked in the wall of the Motee Mahul and enlarged for Wolseley and his men to enter into the courtyard of the palace. With bayonets fixed, they charged through the rooms and drove the enemy out.

Inside the Residency, some of the 90th, who had been besieged since September, held the advance post of the defences. By a pleasing coincidence, Wolseley and his men made contact with their comrades and, much to their joy, the siege was lifted. Expecting to be congratulated and recommended for the Victoria Cross, Captain Wolseley was told by his brigadier that General Campbell was extremely angry that a mere captain of line regiment had broken the siege. Campbell had wanted his favourite 93rd Highlanders to be the first to enter the Residency. Next day, Campbell spotted him and gave him a severe reprimand by asking what he meant by exceeding his instructions. Gradually Campbell's anger thawed but he never recommended Wolseley for the Victoria Cross.

Her Majesty's 7th (Queen's Own) Cavalry was one of the regiments sent to boost the numbers required to bring the mutiny to an end. Rather unusually it was commanded by the Hagart brothers – Colonel Charles and his younger brother, Lieutenant Colonel James Hagart. James Hagart had been newly promoted from major to lieutenant colonel in August 1857 and travelled with the regiment on a three-month voyage on the American-built clipper *Lightning*. Colonel Charles Hagart travelled overland with a veterinary surgeon and two sergeants to select horses for the regiment.

Reaching Allahabad on 7 December, they found that the advance party had procured mounts for the regiment. With effectively only two weeks to break in these wild horses, which had never before had a saddle on them, the regiment joined the march to Cawnpore, where they assembled for the final relief of Lucknow.

Starting out in February 1858, General Sir Colin Campbell's column reached Lucknow in March. After heavy fighting, most of the rebels had escaped due to inept handling of the intended encirclement of the city. Lord Roberts later wrote, 'the campaign which should have then come to an end, was protracted for nearly a year'.

It was learned that a strong force of rebels were in the Musabagh, a large palace and grounds about 4 miles north-west of Lucknow. While the main force attacked the palace, two squadrons of the 7th Cavalry, two guns of the Horse Artillery and a few men of the 78th (Highland) were sent to prevent these rebels escaping. On 19 March, while they halted for a rest and food, a small mud fort or *rezai* in the distance was approached by a small patrol. It appeared to be deserted until its occupants opened fire. The Horse Artillery, along with its cavalry escort, was immediately sent forward to return fire. The effect was to plunge a stick into a hornet's nest. To the astonishment of the soldiers, about fifty sword-brandishing rebels rushed out and charged the guns. Some reports say that the rebels' ferocious behaviour was fuelled by drugs, or they may have been fanatical *ghazis*. The 7th was ordered to charge this mob and were quickly involved in a vicious mêlée. Captain Slade and Lieutenant Wilkin were both severely wounded, leaving young Cornet William Bankes as the only officer. Wilkin later applied for the VC, only to have Edward Pennington dash his application with:

> Another case of refusal is that of Lieutenant Wilkins of (HM) 7th Cavalry and ADC to Sir Hugh Rose in India. This claim was brought forward in August 1863 and founded on the grounds that he had gone to the rescue of a brother officer, the late Cornet Bankes when in peril. Lord Clyde declined to recommend it in 1861, but Sir Hugh Rose recommended it in 1863 and that recommendation was supported by the Horse Guards but it was refused as having already been disposed of in 1861.

Riding a barely broken horse, Bankes became involved in the crowd of *tulwar*-wielding rebels and sword-slashing troopers. He had his revolver, which he fired, hitting three rebels. In the swirl of fighting, a rebel slashed and hamstrung Bankes's horse and Willy fell to the ground. Bankes was immediately set upon by the *tulwars* of the rebels and quickly lost consciousness.

General Sir Hope Grant, in command of the cavalry, wrote:

> Colonel (James) Hagart's gallant attempt to save Bankes who was hacked at by the rebels as he lay disabled on the ground, so far succeeded in that the officer was rescued, though only to die of his wounds a few days later. Colonel Hagart's condition after the mêlée bore the traces of his gallant struggle. His saddle and his horse were slashed about in front and behind, his martingale was divided, his sword-hilt dented, the pocket-handkerchief severed as clearly as with a razor, and a piece of the skin on his right hand cut away.

Sir Hope Grant recommended James Hagart for the Victoria Cross but Sir Colin Campbell declined the application on the grounds that his rank was too high. Instead, he was awarded the Companion of the Bath on 26 July 1858 to compensate for not getting the VC. Hagart, whose courage and quick thinking had saved Willy Bankes's life, wrote to Mrs Bankes: 'He repeatedly told me that he had never suffered at all. That even when he received his wounds he had felt no pain as he had fainted the moment he fell.'

Cornet Bankes, who had only joined the 7th Cavalry the previous spring, was gazetted on 24 December 1858 for the VC. He had been hacked so badly that he was not expected to live. He was taken to the hospital, where his right arm and leg were amputated and other wounds treated. He received the best available treatment from the Surgeon General appointed by Sir Colin Campbell. The latter, impressed by the young cornet's bravery, recommended him for the Victoria Cross, something to which the General did not readily subscribe. Despite the terrible wounds he had received, Bankes appeared to be making a good recovery but, on 6 April 1858, he died of blood poisoning.

Another high-ranking officer who hoped to wear the Victoria Cross was General James Outram. Outram arrived at Cawnpore on 16 September 1857, bringing with him the 90th Light Infantry, the 5th (Northumberland) Fusiliers and a battery of 18-pounders. The force now amounted to 3,179 men, still destined to be outnumbered by the rebels. Although Outram was fully entitled to take over command, he generously allowed General Havelock to complete his task in relieving Lucknow. Outram offered to serve with the Volunteer Cavalry, now numbering 109, a move that Havelock's son, Harry, thought was a way of placing himself in a prominent position to get the Victoria Cross.

During the advance, General Outram, mounted on his huge roan horse, was in the thick of the chase. At Mangalwar, the cavalry was let loose. Wielding a gold-topped Malacca cane, Outram enjoyed his moment with the cavalry as he whipped the fleeing fugitives. The pursuit went on for 8 miles to Bashirhatgani with the rebels losing two guns and 120 men. The volunteer cavalry unanimously voted Outram the Victoria Cross, but he modestly refused on the grounds that he did not deserve it any more than his comrades. An application was submitted to General Colin Campbell, who decided that generals were ineligible. Even when Horse Guards confirmed that it was admissible, Campbell rejected it, thus confirming his reluctance in awarding the Victoria Cross. Adhering to the new Appendix V, Edward Pennington wrote:

> In December 1860, the claims of five officers of the Indian Army and a Warrant Officer were brought forward by the Indian Authorities for various acts of valour during the Mutiny. Although with one exception, these claims were subsequently admitted, they were not recommended by His Royal Highness as they had failed to establish

their claims and His Royal Highness hesitated to recommend the two others to the Secretary of State although submitting Sir Charles Wood's recommendation in their favour. Their cases were, therefore, rejected.

The names, which were notated in the margin, were: Colonel Travers, Lieutenant Colonel Browne, Lieutenant Maclean, Lieutenant Thackeray and Lieutenant Cadell of the Bengal Army, and Conductor Millar, Ordinance Department. This Whitehall game of ping-pong resulted in five receiving the VC, with Lieutenant Maclean being refused. Pennington included in the memo the claim of Lieutenant Colonel Richard Herbert Gall of the HM 14th Hussars for the Cross. His regiment joined General Sir Hugh Rose's Central India Field Force, which took to the field on 8 January 1858.

Having taken the important fortress at Jhansi, Sir Hugh Rose sent the then Major Gall to the fort at Loharri, a few miles away. The fort was square with round towers, surrounded by double ditches and situated on a wide level plain. A company of 3rd Madras Europeans crossed the open space between the village and the fort, taking shelter in a guardhouse close to the ditch. Ignoring the call to surrender, Major Gall ordered a bag of explosives to be lit by the third gate and stormed the fort. The 3rd Europeans rushed in through the smoke and immediately came upon the defenders. Met with a shower of stones and rocks, followed by *tulwar*-wielding rebels, the two sides slugged it out within the close confines of the fort. Finally the rebels were overwhelmed, with the final stand being made at the gateway. A Victoria Cross was awarded to Private Frederick Whirlpool, who received seventeen separate wounds, including one that nearly severed his head from his body. Despite these terrible wounds, he lived until 1899.

Richard Gall applied in 1860 to the Horse Guards for the VC. This was referred back to the Indian Government for further details, which after a delay of two years were supplied by the Commander-in-Chief in December 1862. Upon receipt of these details, the Duke of Cambridge thought there was not sufficient information and turned down the application.

A young officer named John Dartnell of the 86th (Royal County Down) Regiment was commissioned in time for the fighting in the Indian Mutiny. Attached to General Rose's Central column, the 86th and 25th Native Regiment led the attack on Jhansi's 30-foot high walls. Efforts to place the scaling ladders were met by rocks and heavy timbers. Finally, one was successfully placed and Dartnell quickly reached the top of the wall and dropped into a bastion filled with rebels. After parrying the slashing *tulwars* with his sword, Dartnell was overpowered and badly wounded. His left hand was nearly severed and a bullet struck the plate on his sword belt. Fortunately he was saved by his comrades, who forced the rebels from the bastion. For his gallantry, his commanding officer and General Rose recommended him for the Victoria Cross but it was rejected further up the line.

In 1869, Dartnell sold his commission and retired from the Army with the rank of brevet major. After trying his hand at farming in South Africa, Dartnell applied in 1874 to establish the paramilitary Natal Mounted Police Force and saw much action in the 1879 Anglo-Zulu War. Operating in the Anglo-Boer War, he was serving as Major General Sir John Dartnell, and in command of the Imperial Light Horse he saw plenty of action. He retired in 1903 and died in Folkestone in 1913 at the age of 75.

During the years 1850 to 1870, another officer who saw much fighting on the North-West Frontier was Charles Patton Keyes. He was the father of Admiral of the Fleet, Sir Roger Keyes of Zeebrugge fame and grandfather of Geoffrey Keyes VC, who attempted to kill General Rommel in North Africa. Captain Keyes commanded the 1st Punjab Infantry in one of the many punitive expeditions against the tribes on the North-West Frontier. He distinguished himself in a fierce action on 4 May 1860 against the Mahsud Wazirs in the Barara Pass. The Wazirs had blocked the pass with a great *abattis* made of large trees and a series of stone breastworks. Held in reserve, Keyes watched as other Punjab infantry climbed the steep sides only to be driven back by some 5,000 Wazirs. The mountain artillery halted them but the retreating infantry became mixed with Keyes's men. Sir Roger Keyes's account describes his father's action:

> my father shouted to those near him to stand firm and (he) ran forward with drawn sword to meet a Waziri chief who was leading the rush well ahead of his men. A brief hand-to-hand fight took place in full view of the opposing forces, and, having killed the Waziri chief, my father called upon the 1st Punjab Infantry to charge, which they did with such vigour that the Waziris, dismayed by the fall of their leader, turned and fled up the hill, pursued by the 1st P.I., followed by the other two regiments, which, having been rallied by their officers, were spoiling to wipe out their lapse.

The action was decisive and the following day the tribes submitted. General Sir Neville Chamberlain recommended Keyes for the Victoria Cross and was aggrieved when it was rejected. Instead, Keyes received a Brevet Majority.

Sir Roger Keyes went on to describe his father's role on the Umbeyla Expedition of 1863, which was one of the most costly of the 1860s. Sir Neville Chamberlain led 5,000 troops to capture and destroy the village of Malka and drive out the fanatical Pathans who had been raiding other tribes in the region. Unfortunately, one of the victims of these deprivations was the Bunerwal tribe who, fearing a British annexation of their territory, bottled up Chamberlain's force in the Chamia Valley. The troops were overlooked by a steep hill called the Crag Picquet, which dominated the valley. The only problem was that the summit could only be occupied by twelve men. The Crag was fought over many times but on 30 October, Major Keyes led a small detachment to recover it from the Pathans. Sir Roger Keyes wrote about his father's action:

> My father's regiment and a company of Guides Infantry were manning the right flank of the British position. Half an hour before dawn heavy firing was heard in the vicinity of the Crag Picquet, situated on a precipitous hill on the extreme right. My father at once went forward with a small party, to investigate and reinforce the Crag if necessary. … Taking with him an officer and ten of his own men, he proceeded to join them, directing his adjutant, Lieutenant Pitcher, to bring up more men as fast as they could be got together. By dawn he had with him some 75 men at the foot of the rocks, on whom the enemy poured a continuous and heavy fire, hurling down at the same time huge stones, which caused several severe hurts. As soon as it was light enough to distinguish friend from foe, and his left flank was covered by Colonel Brownlow's corps, who moved out into the ravine below, he divided his force into two parties, gave the order to fix swords, and sounded the charge. The Pathans gave a wild shout of 'Allah! Allah!' (in the name of God) and rushed at the Crag, scrambling like cats from rock to rock, by ways through which but one man could pass at a time, in the face of a hot fire and heavy shower of rocks and stones. This daunted some of the men, and Lieutenant Pitcher who was leading at the time being stunned by a heavy stone, but two officers, my father and another, and about twenty-five men, arrived at the summit where they became engaged in an exciting hand-to-hand conflict. My father was severely wounded, but the place was won. The nature of the struggle may be judged from the fact that sixty of the enemy's killed and wounded were left on the Crag.

Charles Keyes wrote in his report:

> From the nature of the approach to the top of the Crag, amongst the large rocks, one or two men could advance at one time, and while

I ascended one path, I directed Lieutenant Fosbery, of the late 4th European Regiment, to push up another, at the head of a few men. He led his party with the greatest coolness and intrepidity, and was the first man to gain the top of the Crag on his side of the attack. Lieutenant Pitcher, equally cool and daring, led a party of men up to the last rock, until he was knocked down and stunned by a large stone thrown from above within a few yards of him.

Roger Keyes tells a different account of what happened:

My father did not mention that he was the first to reach the top of the Crag (some moments before Fosbery arrived by another path), or that he was wounded. As he appeared over the top, three men fired at him from point-blank range. One bullet struck the hilt of his sword and sent it spinning out of his hand, another shattered his left hand and the third made two holes in his *pushteen*, which looked as if the bullet must have passed through his body, but actually it only grazed his side. Feeling for his pistol and not finding it, he remembered loosening his belt while resting before the alarm, and realised that he was unarmed. Fortunately, he was followed by a devoted native officer, Subadar Bahadur Habib Khan, who attacked his assailants and protected him until he recovered his sword.

Lieutenant Colonel A. Wild, commanding the right flank picquets, reported:

The attack upon Crag Picquet, occupied as it was by the enemy in force, was, by the concurrent testimony of all the officers and men who witnessed it, a most daring and brilliant feat of arms, and to Major Keyes is due the credit of not only planning it, but in person he led on his men to the assault, with a perseverance and intrepidity never surpassed.

Major Keyes was gallantly supported by Lieutenant Fosbery and his Adjutant, Lieutenant Henry Pitcher, and I trust that the Brigadier-General will deem the conduct of Major Keyes and his officers deserving of a recommendation to His Excellency the Commander-in-Chief for a reward of gallantry.

Sir Neville Chamberlain wrote in his report dated 31 October 1863 and concluded:

I feel sure that I only anticipate His Excellency's judgement in stating that I consider the capture of the Crag Piquet by Major Keyes a most brilliant exploit. The decision of determination Major Keyes displayed stamp him as possessing some of the highest qualifications of an officer, and I recommend him strongly to His Excellency's favour.

Many recommendations for Major Keyes to receive the Victoria Cross were dashed by the Commander-in-Chief, India, Sir Hugh Rose. Personal gallantry on several occasions during a hard-fought campaign on the part of certain Majors in command of regiments was no more than their duty, and should be recognised by other rewards than the Victoria Cross. ... A captain or a subaltern might stake his life and lose it for the sake of the decoration without playing with the lives of others, but a field officer in command risked not only his life, but possibly the success of the operation devolving upon him, by unnecessary display of personal valour.

With great modesty, Charles Keyes played down his role and put forward Fosbery and Pitcher for the Victoria Cross, which they later received. Keyes received a Brevet Colonel and, in a later expedition, was promoted to brigadier general and received the KCB. He retired in 1884 and was succeeded in his command by Sir Frederick Roberts.

Chapter 3

The Lucknow Defenders
denied the VC

Within days of the outbreak at Meerut, the city of Lucknow was fast becoming the rallying point for the rebels. The events at Cawnpore with the massacre of the men, women and children at Satichaura Ghat and the surviving women and children at Bibighar increased the rebel population in the city as the mutineers arrived from the outlying stations. The same was true of the Residency on the banks of the Gumti River, which was the only place of safety for those living outside Lucknow. Brigadier Sir Henry Lawrence heard of this on 29 June 1857 and sent a force to occupy the grounds and prepare for the defence of the Residency. Small units were sent to out bring in the families of civil servants from outlying towns. The Residency covered some 60 acres of ground and the garrison of 855 officers and soldiers of the 32nd (Cornwall) and 84th (York & Lancaster) regiments, 712 troops of 13th Native Regiment, 153 civilian volunteers with 1,280 non-combatants, including hundreds of women and children. This was increased by some 1,500 survivors of the First Relief Column, which reached the Residency on 25 September. Unable to withdraw, they joined the defenders and waited until November for a larger second relief force to rescue them.

The Residency was in the midst of several palaces and mosques. The buildings that overlooked it were demolished to prevent the rebels getting too close to the defences. Lawrence refused to pull down the mosques to 'spare the holy places'. Unfortunately this well-meaning order meant that the rebel sharpshooters and artillery used these 'holy places' as cover for their bombardment and sniping.

There were nine military and one civilian Victoria Crosses awarded to the garrison during the hellish incarceration in an insanitary and overcrowded makeshift fortress. There were plenty of men who should have been awarded but were either killed or did not think that they warranted the award. The following defenders left it too late to apply.

Lieutenant (now Major) John Bonham of the Bengal Artillery submitted an application in December 1863, some seven years after his action during the Indian Mutiny. His claim landed on the desk of Edward Pennington, a civil servant working for the Permanent Under-Secretary and responsible for the Victoria Cross at the War Office. He had originally been responsible for the Order of the Bath but the new award gave him greater responsibility and not a little stress.

> In these papers claims are put forward to the Victoria Cross on behalf of Major Bonham, Royal (late Bengal) Artillery … for his conduct during the late India Mutiny.
>
> In the case of Major Bonham the claim is advanced of the ground of the courage he displayed on 10 June 1857, at Secora, Oudh in 'remaining with his battery until the last moment and risking his life in the endeavour of recalling the Native Infantry to their allegiance'.
>
> With regard to subsequent conduct at Chinhut, the Committee to whom the claim was referred, with one exception, considered the claim not made out, as he was acting under orders in the course of duty at that time.

As General Lawrence's force struggled back to Lucknow to cross the only available bridge over the Gumti River, the rebel cavalry threatened to outflank them. A charge by thirty-six volunteer cavalrymen threw the rebels into confusion and most of the retreating troops managed to cross. Lawrence ordered a battery of artillery under Lieutenant Bonham to occupy the bridgehead. The problem was they had had no ammunition left but their very presence dissuaded the enemy from approaching and enabled the retreating troops to cross. Mrs Julia Inglis (later Lady Inglis), the wife of Colonel John Inglis, 32nd Regiment, kept a diary during the siege and wrote about Bonham:

> 1 July 1857. Lieutenant Bonham, of the Artillery, supplied the loss of our eight-inch howitzer very ingeniously, by rigging up an eight-inch mortar on to a truck. This proved very useful for throwing shells, howitzer fashion, straight at the enemy, and was nicknamed by the soldiers as 'the Ship'.

She also wrote that Bonham had been wounded twice and:

> was seized with small-pox; he is a very young man, but very clever and most useful artillery officer, so his being laid up was a very great loss.

> 30 August. Mr. Bonham, artillery, was wounded for the third time today, while sitting in the post-office. The wound is a bad one. He had done excellent service.

Edward Pennington continued his report about the twice-promoted Major Bonham:

> It will be seen from the papers that Lord Clyde (Sir Colin Campbell) as far back as 1859, declined to recommend Major Bonham on the grounds that too long a time had elapsed. Major Bonham, however, on whose case the most evidence is laid, preferred his claim on Lord Clyde's successor and his papers referred to the Victoria Cross Committee. They are lost in the Adjutant General's office in Calcutta – copies are processed after a long delay and resubmitted to the Committee, who in December 1863, admit the claim when upwards of 7 years since the performance on which the acts on which the claims are grounded, Lord de Grey is asked to overlook the delay and submit these claims to Her Majesty.
>
> This is another of these cases of perseverance in urging claims in the hope to which his Lordship's attention was called.

The same letter also referred to another claimant: Assistant Surgeon John Lumsdaine, Bombay Medical Service.

> His claim founded of having at the storming of Jhansi, brought in the body of a wounded officer under deadly fire … Assistant Surgeon Lumsdaine was rejected (1859) by the Victoria Cross Committee.

Two more claimants are mentioned in the memo.

> In the cases of Major Edmundstoune and Surgeon Greenhow as far back as 1860, the Horse Guards pointed out the inconvenience of entertaining these claims after so long a period and the proposal of imposing a limit, it appears His Royal Highness should be recommended within a short period of the act having been performed, or it should not be attended to.
>
> In accordance with the decision and yet nearly four years afterwards and still cases of description are being brought forward as if nothing had been written on the subject. If present claims had been submitted at the time, they would probably have been favourably entertained – they are good cases in themselves – as all other cases will, as observed, on Major Edmundstoune claim be again brought forward, if any more Indian Mutiny cases are to be entertained. The grounds on which Major Edmundstoune and Surgeon Greenhow were rejected seem equally applicable in the present instance.

As the survivors of Chinhut retreated to the Residency over the only bridge spanning the Gumti, Lawrence ordered one company of the 32nd (Cornwall), which had not been present at Chinhut, to hold this vital access. It was commanded by Lieutenant (later Major) John Edmundstoune and held the rebels' pressure at bay. Mrs Inglis wrote about Edmundstoune in her diary:

> 20th July. Our casualties are slight, four men killed and twelve wounded, Mr Grant, Mr Hely 7th Cavalry, and Mr Edmundstoune 32nd wounded. This attack and its complete repulse raised our spirits, and gave us confidence that with God's help we should be able to hold on till succour arrive.
>
> 29 September. A very sad day. Very early in the morning a party of men assembled in our yard for a sortie to destroy guns. They were taken from the different regiments, the 32nd furnishing a good number. Mr. McCabe was told off to lead. John (Inglis) protested against the selection, saying he had already led three sorties, and it was not fair to take him again; but General Outram said he must have him. The affair was far from being successful; only seven guns were spiked, and our loss was most severe. Poor Mr. McCabe was carried past our door shot through the lungs. Mr. Lucas, a gentleman volunteer, mortally wounded; Major Simmonds, 5th Fusiliers killed, Mr. Edmonstoune, 32nd, slightly wounded. The latter behaved most bravely, having with three of the 32nd rushed forward to spike a gun when a good many of the others fell back; he and two of the men were hit, the remaining one spiked the gun – an act worthy of the V.C. Cuney and Smith of the 32nd were both killed: two braver men never lived; the former had no right to be out, as he was on the sick-list, but he could not resist accompanying the party, as his comrade Smith and he had been together all through the siege.
>
> 7th October. Mr Edmundstoune, 32nd, had tea with us and a long gossip principally about his home; he was looking rather pulled down from the wound in his head; it was his second, and he knew if he had a third it would be a very bad one; he seemed quite superstitious about it. He said he had heard that news had gone to England of our garrison being all cut up, which grieved us much; one of our saddest thoughts during the siege was the reflection of how those we love the most must be suffering. How one used to long to hear something of them!

In a note written in 1864, Pennington referred to the number of men of the 32nd (Cornwall) who had applied for the VC.

> There are several cases on record in which the grant of the Cross has been refused. For acts performed during the Indian Mutiny.
>
> In October 1859, the claimant of one officer and 11 non-commissioned officers of the 32nd Regiment and the same regiment

as Lieutenant Edmundstoune were submitted to the General Commander in Chief by Lieutenant Colonel Lowe, the commanding officer, for acts of gallantry as performed as in his case at Lucknow in September 1857. Three only of these claimants were, however, recommended to the Secretary of State and admitted. His Royal Highness, declining to recommend the rest, although concurring with the Board of Officers who investigated these acts to the high merit of all the individuals concerned.

The claim of Lieutenant Edmundstoune is now brought under the Secretary of State's notice for the first time. It would appear from the papers submitted that the case was brought before the Horses Guards in 1860 at the same time as that of Captain Aitkin of the Bengal Army by the late Sir John Inglis, but it was refused at that time. Because it had not been received through the Commander in Chief in India. In March 1863, by Sir Hugh Rose and the Indian Government received the Cross on the recommendation of Her Royal Highness for his repeated acts of gallantry at Lucknow which appear to have been conspicuous.

In a 19 May 1862 reply to a letter from Major Edmundstoune, Major General Sir John Inglis, his old commander, wrote from the Citadel in Corfu:

> I am sorry to find from your letter that you are thinking of leaving the 32nd and if my opinion of you as an officer in any way procures your employment I should not only be glad to do so, but I feel it a duty I owe to you.
>
> As a Company officer you were always zealous and had a thorough knowledge of your duty in every respect. In the field it is sufficient for me to say – I thoroughly recommend you for the Victoria Cross for which I consider you were justly entitled for your conduct in command of a portion of your company in taking a gun at the Iron Bridge Lucknow.
>
> Your conduct on all occasions whether in the Field or Quarters was everything I could wish.
>
> Lady Inglis desires her kind regards and remember me to all the old hands.

Edmundstoune wrote at the same time to Lieutenant Colonel James Carmichael of the 32nd, who replied in much the same way as Sir John Inglis, stating that the lieutenant was a fine officer who conducted himself well. Sadly, Sir John died just five months later.

Edmundstoune also requested the newly promoted Lieutenant Colonel Granville Stapylton of 32nd Regiment to forward copies to the Horse Guards in which his sponsors supported his claim for the Victoria Cross. Lieutenant Edmundstoune also submitted two testimonies from men under his command at Lucknow. The letters were written by Edmundstoune, with the first by Private Bryan Devine, who stated:

> I was sent on 30 June 1857 with Lieutenant Edmundstoune when he defended the Iron Bridge over the River Gumti to cover the retreat from Chinhut. After occupying the bridge and ordering his party to lie down, he himself crossed over to reconnoitre; He was fired at by several of the enemy: he sent a file of men who accompanied him (one of whom was wounded) back to the party at the double – he retiring slowly over the bridge by himself. While retiring he was fired at several times but still continued to walk steadily and coolly. When we were ordered to retire into the Garrison, he brought in the men steadily in perfect order, walking himself about 15 yards behind the men.
>
> On 29 September 1857, I also accompanied Lieutenant Edmundstoune when he led a sortie of ten men of his Company. We took six guns and two mortars, destroying the carriage of the fifth and bursting the sixth – a 24 lb iron gun. From five of these guns placed singly in different parts of the street, we received a discharge of grape.
>
> Lieutenant Edmundstoune was the leading man at all these guns. We lost a number of men. Signed Bryan Devine. Private. 32nd Regiment.

The other testimony came from Corporal Henry A. Brett:

> I was out with Lieutenant Edmundstoune on 29 September 1857, when he led a sortie of ten men of the Company. We took and destroyed by spiking and bursting six guns and two mortars. From five of these guns which were placed singly in different parts of the street, we received a round of grape. As we approached, Lieutenant Edmundstoune was in the lead of each of these guns. We suffered severely when we retired into the Residency and Lieutenant Edmundstoune was severely wounded while we were retiring.
>
> Private Devine and I are now the only men in the Regiment present on that occasion. Signed H.A. Brett. Corporal. 32nd Regiment.

All these letters and testimonies were sent forward to Edward Pennington, who submitted them to the Awards Committee.

Pennington then addressed the case of Captain Aitkin, late of the 13th Native Infantry. His conduct during the Lucknow siege resulted in a five-part citation, which was published some six years after the event. Dated 17 April 1863, it reads: 'For various acts of gallantry performed during the defense of the Residency of Lucknow from June 30th to November 22nd 1857.'

Aitken was mentioned in despatches ten times and appears in Colonel John Inglis's reports:

> Lieutenant Aitken, with the whole of the 13th NI, which remained to us, with the exception of the Sikhs, commanded the Baillie Guard, perhaps the most important position in the whole of the defenses. With respect to the native troops, I am of the opinion that their loyalty has never been surpassed. They were indifferently fed and worse housed. They were exposed, especially the 13th Regiment, under the gallant Lieutenant Aitken, to a most galling fire of round shot and musketry, which materially decreased their numbers. They were so near the enemy that conversation could be carried out between them, and every effort, persuasion, promise, and threat was alternatively resorted to in vain, to seduce them from their allegiance to the handful of Europeans, who, in all probability would have been sacrificed by their desertion.

On the evening of the relief, a work party of Aitken's men had been led out to level a rebel's battery. Suddenly they were attacked by the advancing 78th Highlanders who, mistaking Aitken's *sepoys* for rebels, charged them with the bayonet. Aitken rushed up, crying, 'For God's sake, don't harm these poor fellows. They've saved all our lives!' Fortunately, only three sepoys were wounded.

Aitken not only had to wait an excessive time for his Cross to be approved, but the actual presentation was something of a farce. Although it had taken six years for his award to be gazetted, Aitken had to wait a further two years before its presentation in May 1865. This was due to the Commander-in-Chief, General Sir Hugh Rose, breaking his ribs in a hunting accident and delaying his tour of inspection. In May 1865, he and his staff arrived in Lucknow to present Major Robert Aitken, now with the Oudh Police, with his long-overdue VC.

Pennington was still dealing with the problem of Major Edmundstoune's application.

> Nothing, however, was said about Major Edmunstoune at that time but that Officer, that finding that Captain Aitkin had been awarded the Cross, obtained the advocacy of Lord Melville, the Colonel of the Regiment and through the commanding officer of the Regiment the case is now sent through to Sir Hugh Rose. This is apparently one of the cases of perseverance alluded in the Horse Guards letter of 1860 and it must be remembered that men of the same Regiment have been admitted to have been of high

merit who distinguished themselves at the same time and place have been rejected, moreover. The person who held the office of Commander in Chief at the time of the HEIC occurrence is now dead and the same weight cannot attach to the recommendation of the present holder of the office, however distinguished he may be. Hence the inconvenience for these claims being brought forward so long afterwards.

Two years were considered a sufficient time to allow after the close of the Crimean War it is now 6 to 7 years since the occurrences and the reasons given in December 1860 for putting a limit on the period for bringing forward these claims and must apply with greater force in March 1864.

A note was written from Horse Guards on 22 November 1864 with a copy of a letter from the India Office forwarding recommendations from the Commander-in-Chief and the Government of India for the Victoria Cross to be awarded to Major John Bonham and Assistant Surgeon John Lumsdaine.

> The act of gallantry for which Surgeon Lumsdaine is recommended for the decoration at the storming of Jhansi under Sir Hugh Rose's observation, and as the Government of India and Sir Charles Wood concur in the merit of the Service rendered, His Royal Highness begs to recommend to Earl de Grey and Ripon the cases of these two officers who he considers well deserving of the Victoria Cross.

Surgeon Goodhow persisted with his claim, and in 1864, resubmitted his application for the Victoria Cross. A Minute Paper was sent by Pennington to Lord Lugard in which he submits the wording of the claim by Surgeon Goodhow:

> Here is another claim for the Victoria Cross on behalf of Surgeon Goodhow of the Bengal Medical Service, who is recommended for having, 'on 25 September 1857, voluntarily left the Residence, Lucknow during the night – and at great personal risk, brought in some 12 to 15 soldiers who would in all probability [have] perished'.

25 September was the date when the First Relief Force fought their way through the narrow streets of the city to reach the Residency, losing many men to gunfire from the building along the route. Pennington went on:

> The conduct of this officer was highly spoken of, but the grounds on which the recent case of Major Edmundstoune was rejected are equally applicable in the present instance. It is now six or seven years since these acts of bravery were performed for which it is proposed in this instance that the high distinction should be conferred and

bearing in mind the inconvenience which results in entertaining at long intervals after the performance of acts of bravery.

As pointed out in your letter dated 18th December 1860, Lord de Grey can only express his regrets.

Lord de Grey wrote on the memo sent by Pennington:

I do not doubt for a moment that this Doctor has been recommended for the Victoria Cross by competent authority in 1857 when the act was performed and any objection would have been raised – but after an interval of four years, he apparently makes up his mind that he ought to have the decoration – in 1861 applies for it through a Surgeon Major, who together with another Doctor appear to be the only witnesses who can bear testimony of difficulty and danger as described by Doctor Bird – if this act was described as worthy of a Cross by Surgeon Major Johnson, he might have thought to have reported it to the Officer in Command or even to have represented it to Sir James Outram or other Senior Officers of the force who must have heard of this act if it occurred – I do not think the Warrant contemplated the bestowal of the decoration for an act brought forward at this late period.

He then went on with the fact that Greenhow did not go out alone, but men of the 84th Regiment who had fought their way to the Residency went out into the streets to bring in their wounded comrades. He went on to write:

Besides the men who accompanied Dr. Greenhow, soldiers of the 84th (York & Lancaster) Regiment, who carried the wounded men into safety or the others with horses went to bring in the wounded and are quite as much entitled to claim the Cross as the Doctor – and no doubt, if alive or wounded, do so when they heard that the Doctor got it.

Under all circumstances I do not think there is definite evidence as to the conditions of the act to grant the claimant for the Cross.

In 1864, Pennington wrote to the four claimants:

Under the circumstances, Lord de Grey expresses his regret that it is impossible at this distant date to bring under Her Majesty's notice the claims that the officers brought forward.

Chapter 4

Not Before the Enemy

The next addition was Appendix VI, covering the *Cases of Conspicuous Courage and Bravery Displayed under Circumstances of Danger but not before the Enemy*. This new warrant was not popular with the Whitehall civil servants. The Clerk at the War Office, Edward Pennington, described it as 'an inconvenient precedent'. He commented that it 'would be making the Victoria Cross too cheap to grant it'. In fact, it was never published in the *London Gazette* and was something of a guilty secret. The event that caused the warrant to be altered was the dramatic fire at sea and outstanding bravery of the troops on the SS *Sarah Sands*.

The *Sarah Sands* was named after the wife of the Liverpool mayor and was only the second screw propeller-driven steamship in the world after the *Great Eastern*. Built as a sailing ship, she had two coal-powered engines and an iron bulkhead, which divided the ship into three watertight compartments. She was chartered by the Royal Navy to take the 54th Regiment to India as reinforcements for the depleted number of British regulars. She was chosen to carry the 54th (West Norfolk), but the ship was found unfit to carry that number, so they were split between three ships. On the *Sarah Sands* were 368 officers and men, eight women including officers' wives, and the daughters of the commanding officer, Colonel Bowland Moffat. Leaving England on 15 August 1857, the passengers endured a slow journey to Cape Town, during which they ran low on water and food. Several members of the crew were arrested for mutiny and clapped in irons before being imprisoned in Cape Town. Captain James Castle of *Sarah Sands* later wrote: 'They had no alternative but to make up the complement of the crew with such as presented themselves, and who were nearly all foreigners.'

By 11 November, they were about 800 miles from Mauritius and 600 miles from Ceylon, having lost the foremast in a violent squall on 7 November. It was then that a sergeant noticed smoke coming from a hatch at the stern. Captain Castle stopped the engine and manoeuvred the ship so she headed into the wind, allowing the smoke to blow over the stern. The soldiers were mustered on deck and instructed to clear the magazines of gunpowder. Boats were then lowered into the rough sea and women, children, the sick and younger drummer boys were loaded aboard. One boat was noticeable as it carried Colonel Moffat and his family. Most of the scratch crew took to the boats and it was left to the soldiers to try to douse the flames.

While hoses played water on the burning stores in the hold, the most immediate threat came from the two powder-filled magazines. There were ninety barrels in each magazine. The soldiers braved the smoke and carried the barrels to the rail and dropped them overboard. On the port magazine the task was more difficult but the troops managed to clear all but one or two barrels.

There were many acts of courage that day including retrieving the regimental colours from the burning part of the ship. They stood at the end of the smoke-filled saloon, clamped against the partition. Two officers tried to retrieve them but were overcome with smoke. The ship's quartermaster put a wet cloth over his face and succeeded in freeing the colours but collapsed through smoke inhalation. Private Wiles managed to enter and drag the crewman and colours out into fresh air.

About 9.00 pm, the expected explosion blew out the port stern. By this time the ship was a mass of flame. Thanks to the watertight bulkheads, the ship was still afloat. Captain Castle ordered one crew playing water on the bulkhead to keep it cool while the soldiers pulled their comrades from the smoke. At 10.00 pm, the main topsail caught fire and six men climbed aloft with wet blankets to extinguish the flames, but it was to no avail as the mast was almost burnt through.

Throughout the night, the flames were gradually dampened down and by morning the ship was a smouldering wreck. The after part had been blown out and 15 feet of seawater filled the hold. The morning was spent baling and pumping out the water. Captain Castle used spare sails and blankets to plug the holes in the ship. By now it was safe for the boats to come alongside and the women and children were taken back on board. Another night and day was spent pumping water out of the ship. Then, about 5.00 pm on the 13th, sails were improvised and the *Sarah Sands* began her laborious journey back to Mauritius. It was a slow and uncomfortable journey until the 23rd when they reached the island, where they were greeted with enthusiasm by the population. The 54th spent six weeks on Mauritius before completing their passage to Calcutta.

In the aftermath came the rewards. The Royal Humane Society honoured Captain Castle and, bizarrely, Colonel Moffat, who spent most of the fire sitting in a boat several hundred yards away. Moffat was not censured but did lose the command of the regiment to newly promoted Lieutenant Colonel William Brett. Lieutenant Houston wrote to his brother: 'So the Royal Humane Society have determined to give our Chief a Medal! What a farce it will appear when they know the true facts. The East India Company have, I hear, given Captain Castle £1000 – not bad.'

Captain Castle became a national hero and he was offered a command of a mail steamer with the Peninsular and Oriental Steam Navigation Company. On 29 January 1858, General Sir Colin Campbell wrote to the Horse Guards:

> I am not sure that the Statutes of the Victoria Cross admit officers and men whom he [William Brett] recommends being honoured with that Decoration. I am sure, however, that no men in conflict with an enemy have ever deserved to be more conspicuously marked out than those composing the 54th Regt where, to use the words of Major Brett, they determined to fight the fire inch by inch in the burning ship.

This led to the warrant being altered to include bravery not in the face of the enemy. Major Brett had been in command of the men aboard the burning ship and in an interview with the Adjutant General he pleaded the case for a Victoria Cross to be conferred on the regiment. Instead, Horse Guards insisted that a VC should be awarded to an individual. Brett wrote in August 1860 recommending Private Andrew Walsh and citing the following instance of gallantry:

> For having, soon after the outbreak of the Fire, when volunteers were called for to clear the Powder Magazine, entered the Powder Magazine and with other soldiers of 54th Regiment succeeded in clearing it of the greater portion of the powder. He did not quit the Magazine 'til from fire and smoke it was impossible to remain, thus rendering invaluable service.
>
> For having, in company with Mr Welsh (Chief Officer of the *Sarah Sands*) gone aloft with wet blankets, and succeeded in extinguishing the fire at the main top-sail yard (the yard and mast being on fire) a service of great peril and risk, the ship at the time rolling heavily and being as stated by Capt Castle in his report 'one body of flame from stern to the main rigging'.
>
> And generally – after the imminent danger during the many hours the fire lasted had been overcome – for general conduct and example during twelve days (a period of great anxiety and danger) the wreck was at sea before reaching Mauritius.

This was followed by a letter from the regiment's commander, Colonel Charles Michel, further recommending Andrew Walsh for the Victoria Cross. Many officers and men on the *Sarah Sands* were outraged at the negative response by the War Office. Thanks to the intransigence of the Civil Service, who wanted this Appendix scrapped, they searched for loopholes to deny the men on the burning ship any awards.

In the event, the *Sarah Sands* incident paved the way for two future 'not in the face of the enemy' acts but did not include Private Andrew Walsh. In a typically bureaucratic manner it was decided that no awards were to be made for the *Sarah Sands* as it was judged to be retrospective because the warrant had not been altered before the incident had taken place. This appeared to be unjust as the Appendix for the eligibility of members of the military forces of the Honourable East India Company was backdated in order to accept the Persian War VCs from 1856.

The new Appendix VI brought a fresh crop of applicants, including a letter written in 1862 from Lieutenant Joseph Bourke of 29th (Worcestershire), previously serving in the West India Regiment. He recommended himself for the Victoria Cross for his part in extinguishing an ammunition magazine fire at Fort Charlotte, Bahamas. On 8 January 1860, the men of the companies of the 1st West India Regiment stationed at Nassau swiftly dealt a fire that broke out at Fort Charlotte, and the following Garrison Order was published on the subject:

> Lieutenant-Colonel Bourchier takes the earliest opportunity in his power of expressing his thanks to Major R. D'O. Fletcher, the officers, the non-commissioned officers, and the men of the 1st West India Regiment, for the prompt manner in which they turned out and lent their efforts to avert the extension of the late fire at Fort Charlotte.
>
> Such occasions as this test the discipline of a corps in a high degree, the more so when, as in the present instance, the danger of an explosion from the proximity of the flames to the magazine was imminent.
>
> Where all were zealous, the conduct of Ensign Bourke, 1st West India Regiment, was most conspicuous, who, assisted by Company Sergeant-Major Mason and a party of four men of the regiment, placed wet blankets on the most exposed portion of the roof of the magazine, which was then actually ignited; and it will be most gratifying to Lieutenant-Colonel Bourchier to bring the circumstance under the notice of H.R.H. the General Commanding-in-Chief.

Bourke felt that as Appendix VI was now in force, he was justified in applying for the Victoria Cross. The Adjutant General's office checked the regimental diary and found that the fire had virtually burned itself out and that Bourke was in no danger. He had to make do with a mentioned in despatches.

The two incidents where the Victoria Cross was applied were in the mid-1860s. The first was Private Timothy O'Hea of the Rifle Regiment who put out a fire in the ammunition wagon on a train in Canada. The other was an excessive award of five VCs battling heavy surf for a rescue in an open boat off the Andaman Islands. The men involved were Surgeon Campbell Mellis Douglas, who was an expert boatman, and his crew of Privates David Bell, James Cooper, William Griffiths and Thomas Murphy – all from the 24th (Warwickshire) Regiment.

One of the least documented officer VCs was that of Captain Andrew Scott. Early in 1877, men of the Indian Army marched into the small dusty settlement of Quetta and set up a cantonment in the face of intense hostility from the largely Muslim Pathans. The garrison embarked on a building programme in anticipation of housing a force that could be used against the Afghan ruler, Sher Ali. Despite the undercurrent of resentment from the local inhabitants, the British employed many Pathans as labourers. On the evening of 26 July, three local Kakar Pathans attacked Royal Engineer Lieutenants Hewson and Kunhardt, who were overseeing building operations of the new Residency. In a frenzied knife attack, Hewson was killed and Kunhardt badly wounded. A soldier of the 4th Sikhs rushed up and defended the stricken Kunhardt but in doing so, lost his life.

Captain Scott, who was drilling his men nearby, heard the commotion and dashed to the scene followed by some of his men. Grabbing a rifle with fixed bayonet from one of his men, Scott killed two of the murderers. He then got into a tussle with the third man, who managed to wound Scott, but his men arrived close behind and made short work of the assailant.

Scott was recommended for the Victoria Cross, the last time one was awarded for gallantry not in the face of the enemy. There is a lack of documentary evidence about his VC, which while timely, seems hardly to merit the highest award. On 18 January 1878, his citation was published in the *London Gazette* and he received his Cross on 15 April that year, although there is no record of an investiture.

This 'inconvenient precedent' was solved with the creation of the Albert Medal in 1866, designed to cover those who 'in saving or endeavouring to save the lives of others from shipwreck or other peril of the sea, endangered their own lives'. In 1881, Appendix VI was quietly dropped.

Chapter 5

Civilians Refused the Cross

The use of civilian volunteers under the command of the military was prevalent during the Indian Mutiny. The slow build-up of Her Majesty's regiments in reaching India by ship took up to six months to complete. It became necessary to use the male civilians employed by the Indian Civil Service as volunteers to augment the professional military.

The exploits of Thomas Kavanagh, Ross Mangles and William McDonell were pushed by the East India Company in the hope that they would be awarded the Victoria Cross. On 13 December 1858, Appendix VII altered the warrant by 'Extending Eligibility for the Victoria Cross to Non-Military Persons Bearing Arms as Volunteers'. In the case of these three civilians, they did not bear arms. In sequence, Kavanagh acted as a guide at Lucknow; Mangles carried a wounded soldier for many miles through swampy ground; and McDonell cut through a rope on a small boat under heavy fire.

The wording, which covered only the Indian Mutiny, stated:

> and during the progress of the operations which We have undertaken against the Insurgent Mutineers in India, it has not infrequently happened that non-military persons who have borne arms as volunteers against the mutineers both at Lucknow and elsewhere have performed deeds of gallantry in consideration of which they are not according to the strict provisions of Our first recited Warrant eligible for this high distinction.

There was a fourth civilian VC, the curiously named George Bell Chicken. Born on 2 March 1833 in Howden Pans, Northumberland, he had risen to chief officer on an East India sailing ship. When he was in Calcutta at the start of the Indian Mutiny, he volunteered for the Indian Naval Brigade. He is probably the only naval member to have won his Victoria Cross on horseback, when he attacked a superior force, killing five, before being rescued by mounted Sikhs. He was gazetted on 27 April 1860 but died at sea before he was invested with his Victoria Cross.

There were to be other civilians who laid claim for the Victoria Cross during Queen Victoria's reign. One such civilian was the Reverend James Adams, the epitome of a 'muscular Christian'. As a young Divinity student, he was described as 'the strongest man in Ireland'. Ordained in the Church of England, he travelled to India and joined the East India Company's Bengal establishment. He came to the attention of the deeply religious General Frederick Roberts, who chose him to be a member of his Staff of the Kabul Field Force. There is a well-known photograph of Roberts and his Staff with James Adams seated on the ground before him.

On 11 December 1879, at Killa Kazi, outside Kabul, General Roberts miscalculated the strength of the Afghan army. Instead of the expected 2,000, there were some 25,000 warriors swiftly closing in on Roberts's force. As the British cavalry retreated in the face of overwhelming odds, Roberts wrote in his report:

> Our Chaplain who had accompanied me throughout the day, behaved in this particular place with conspicuous gallantry. Seeing a wounded man of the 9th Lancers staggering towards him, Adams dismounted, and tried to lift the man to his own charger. Unfortunately, the mare broke loose and was never seen again. Adams, however, managed to support the Lancer until he was able to make him over to some of his comrades.
>
> Adams rejoined me in time to assist two more of the 9th Lancers who were struggling under their horses at the bottom of a ditch. He was an unusually powerful man, and by sheer strength dragged the Lancers clear of their horses. The Afghans, meanwhile, had reached Bhagwana and were so close to the ditch that I thought my friend, the padre, could not possibly escape. I called out to him to look after himself, but he paid no attention to my warnings until he had pulled the almost exhausted Lancers to the top of the slippery bank.

This does seem to be an exaggeration as the ditch was full of water. Yet Adams was reported as being 'up to his waist in water' but was still able to rescue the men, who, trapped beneath their horses, must have been in danger of drowning. Nevertheless, Roberts wrote to the Adjutant General in India on 29 January 1880, recommending James Adams for the Victoria Cross in the full knowledge that there was no precedent for a clergyman winning the award. On 11 May, this recommendation went before the Military Department of the Government of India, who responded:

> In the opinion of the Government of India the precedents established in 1857 when the VC was conferred on Messrs Mangles and McDonell … and Mr Kavanagh … would be applicable to the case of Mr Adams. … The circumstance of that gentleman's position as a non-combatant and a clergyman do, in the opinion of the Government, mark the character of his gallantry in a special and remarkable manner.

On receipt at the War Office of the fulsome recommendation from India, the Military Secretary, Lieutenant General Sir Edmund Whitmore, tersely rejected it.

> The Revd J.W. Adams is not eligible for the decoration in question as it appears that he holds no Military Commission. The cases of Kavanagh, Mangles & McDonnell do not constitute a precedent in as much as the decoration was conferred on these gentlemen by a special Warrant.

Frederick Roberts's star was in the ascendancy after his own successful Afghan exploits. The weight of British public opinion was with him as well as the favour of Queen Victoria, so that Whitmore had little alternative but to accede to Roberts's determination to see his respected chaplain's gallantry rewarded.

He wrote stating that if the present warrant did not allow Adams to receive the VC, why not draw up a new warrant? This was readily endorsed by the India Office and, although it had never been suggested before, had the desired effect. On 6 August 1881, Queen Victoria approved a new category – Appendix X – 'Warrant Extending for the Victoria Cross to the Indian Ecclesiastical Establishments'. For the first and only time was a warrant specifically made for one individual, and the odds of anyone else being eligible were nil.

Another fleeting candidate for the Victoria Cross was the war correspondent Archibald Forbes. He reported many of the battles from the Franco-Prussian War, the Balkan Wars to the Afghan War, and was regarded as the most intrepid and colourful of newsmen. Awarded with twelve foreign decorations for the wars he reported for the *Daily News*, he received none from his home country. Arriving from Afghanistan, he reported the final months of the Anglo-Zulu War.

Forbes had been highly critical of Lord Chelmsford, the charming but ineffectual Commander of the British Army in South Africa. After the final battle at the Zulu capital of Ulundi, all the correspondents then set about writing up their notes or completing their sketches. Forbes approached Lord Chelmsford and requested that his report should be included in the despatches he felt sure were leaving shortly. Having a short fuse and a dislike for Chelmsford, he was irritated by the General's reply that he would not risk sending a courier with the news of the victory until the following day. He pointed out, not unreasonably, that the countryside was still full of roaming bands of Zulus and it was too dangerous. Forbes was outraged and blurted out, 'Then, sir, I will start myself at once.'

Afterwards he admitted he was sorry for himself the moment he had spoken. With the nearest telegraph some 100 miles away at Landman's Drift, it seemed a foolish act of bravado. The gamblers amongst his acquaintances started placing bets and insisted on taking Forbes's £5 stake as he was not expected to be seen again. In a generous act, Forbes carried sketches and some staff messages before setting off at dusk.

> It was somewhat gruesome work, that first stretch through the sullen gloom of the early night, as I groped my way through the rugged bush trying to keep to the trail of the wagon wheels. I could see the dark figures of the Zulus against the blaze of the fires in the destroyed kraals to the right and to the left of my track, and their shouts came to me on the still night air. At length I altogether lost my way, and there was no resource but to halt until the moon should rise and show me my whereabouts. The longest twenty minutes I have ever spent in my life was while sitting on my trembling horse in a little glade of the bush, my hand on the butt of my revolver, waiting for the moon's rays to flash down into the hollow. At length they came; I discerned the right direction, and in half an hour I was inside the reserve camp of Etoganeni imparting the tidings to a circle of eager listeners. The great danger was past.

Forbes really was taking a chance for only recently an officer and trooper had been killed on the same track. Using the fortified posts that had been established to protect the column's line of supply, Forbes was able to change horses six times. Artillery Lieutenant Henry Curling was stationed at Fort Marshall and wrote to his mother:

> Forbes the correspondent got here at daylight having ridden all night through dangerous country. He hopes to get to the end of the wire about 50 miles off this evening. Anyhow, he is far ahead of all the other correspondents. He is a great, strong, coarse looking man able to undergo any amount of fatigue and to put up with any amount of snubbing. These specials are a terrible nuisance. They expect to be welcomed everywhere and in fact come whether you

welcome them or not. One feels at the same time that it is dangerous to be uncivil to them. They are obliged to be pushing, unsnubbable men; no others would get on at all.

At about 3.00 pm the following day, an exhausted and dishevelled Forbes reached Landman's Drift, having travelled 110 miles in twenty hours. The telegraph had just been extended to the Cape so news now reached London within twenty-four hours. Having sent his report, Forbes rode on to Durban, where he mailed his full story. Incredibly, he had ridden 295 miles in just fifty-five hours!

Forbes's report was the first to reach Britain and was read out in both Houses of Parliament. It brought him even greater fame and his exploit came to be known as 'The Ride of Death'. There was even a suggestion that he should receive the Victoria Cross. More modestly, Forbes applied for the campaign medal to add to his impressive collection of foreign awards. It was Lord Chelmsford who firmly blocked this award as Forbes had not carried the official report and the telegrams he had carried were of a more personal nature.

Another journalist who did receive the Victoria Cross was Viscount Fincastle, or the Right Honourable Alexander Edward Murray. He had joined the British Army in 1891 but had taken an extended leave in 1897. He was appointed as a special war correspondent for *The Times* to report the progress of the Malakand Field Force on the North-West Frontier.

At Nawa Kili on 7 August, two of the better mounted horsemen broke away ahead of their colleagues. They were Captain H.T.E. Palmer, who commanded one of the squadrons, and Lieutenant R.T. Greaves, on leave from the Lancashire Fusiliers and who had been given permission to go to the front as a war correspondent for several Indian papers.

Three other officers – Lieutenant Colonel Adams of the Guides, Lieutenant MacLean commanding a party of *sowars,* and Viscount Fincastle, in the field as a war reporter, noticed the plight of Palmer and Greaves who were being attacked by the Afghan tribesmen. Adams and Fincastle immediately galloped to the rescue, while MacLean momentarily stayed behind to organise his men into good fire positions. Then he, too, galloped off with five *sowars* to support his fellow officers. While Adams and Fincastle were riding strongly to save Palmer and Greaves, the tribesmen fell back a little but then opened fire, killing Fincastle's horse. MacLean arrived soon after and as he helped to lift the mortally wounded Greaves onto his horse, he was shot through both thighs, severing his femoral arteries. Pulling him to shelter, his comrades could do nothing for him and he bled to death.

Robert Adams and Viscount Fincastle were recommended for the Victoria Cross by the Field Force Commander, Sir Bindon Blood. A technicality arose in the case of the latter. Lieutenant Viscount Alexander Fincastle was not serving under Sir Bindon; he was on leave from his own unit and accompanying the expedition on condition that he was a civilian correspondent and should not be eligible for any medal. Fortunately these points were sidestepped and Sir Bindon found a way by fictitiously attaching Fincastle as ADC to Lord Elgin, the Indian Viceroy. This enabled Viscount Fincastle to receive the Malakand campaign medal as well as the Victoria Cross.

Another journalist with aspirations of becoming a politician was Winston Spencer Churchill. He had accompanied the Malakand Field Force and the Tirah Expedition as a young officer in the 4th Hussars and ridden in the charge of the 21st Lancers at Omdurman. Brigadier Jeffries recognised his 'courage and resolution' in rescuing a wounded man in the Malakand expedition.

Resigning his commission he went to South Africa to report for the *Morning Post* on the Boer War. He was the most richly rewarded of all the correspondents who reported from the Boer War. Always on the lookout for some dangerous assignment, Churchill travelled on an armoured train, which he described as: 'Nothing looks more formidable and impressive than an armoured train, but nothing is, in fact, more vulnerable and helpless.'

The train had been sent to reconnoitre the Boer positions near Colenso and to find if the track had been destroyed. On 15 November 1900, the train was derailed near Chieveley and attacked. The escort was composed of half a company of Dublin Fusiliers and another half company of Dublin Light Infantry. The Boers were waiting and the train derailed. The driver and another officer reported that Churchill behaved bravely in helping the wounded. He was captured, sent to Pretoria but escaped – by rail. Sir Ian Hamilton proposed that Churchill should receive the Victoria Cross but this was quickly quashed by General Buller, who disliked Hamilton and the 'pushy' Churchill. Those in higher authority decided that Churchill was 'a medal hunter prepared to display reckless gallantry which is also tactically justified to earn his reward'. It did not matter to the young Churchill, for his exploits lifted him into the political arena.

Another person recommended for the Victoria Cross at the time of the Fincastle episode was Francis Berkley Henderson, a former Royal Navy lieutenant who, in 1884, was invalided out of the service. From 1895 to 1896, he was employed by the Colonial Office as Secretary to the Governor of the Gold Coast before being appointed Travelling

Commissioner of the Gold Coast Colony. Henderson led a small expedition against the most powerful slave-dealing chieftain in the area: Alimani Samori of the Sofas. Leading large armies equipped with modern weapons, he raided throughout what is now northern Ghana. A message was sent to Samori that the British would take reprisals against him if he did not stop slave raiding.

Francis Henderson had moved into in the northern Gold Coast and established a position at Dawkita on the border with the Ivory Coast. Henderson had only a small force comprising George Ferguson, an African surveyor, a native police officer and forty-one constables from the Gold Coast Constabulary. Learning that the Sofas were approaching, Henderson, with George Ferguson's help, fortified three native compounds and waited for reinforcements. In one of the epic actions of the Victorian era, the defence of Dawkita is all but forgotten.

Soon Henderson's small force was besieged by an army of 7,000 Sofas, outnumbered 160 to 1. The fighting lasted for four days and nights with the defenders losing only two men killed and nine wounded. The losses among the Sofas was estimated at more that 400. With ammunition running low, Henderson decided to evacuate the town and retire to Wa on the other bank of the Volta River, where he could expect reinforcements. Leaving at night, Henderson's small force met up with fifty reinforcements and two guns. Henderson employed his diplomatic skills when he approached the enemy camp to negotiate. He was kept captive for two weeks as he negotiated with the Sofa chiefs and finally gained their approval to evacuate his men back to the coast.

It was a minor action but one that piqued Queen Victoria's interest and there was talk of a Victoria Cross being awarded. It was pointed out by the Military Secretary that, despite Francis Henderson's gallantry in the face of overwhelming odds, he was not eligible for either the Victoria Cross or the Distinguished Service Order as he was a civilian. The matter was passed to the Admiralty, who considered that, as he was a retired Royal Navy officer, he would be eligible for the DSO. Supported by the Colonial Office, Henderson was duly gazetted on 8 March 1898.

Another attempt to have a civilian awarded the Victoria Cross was made during the 1900 Boxer Rebellion. The Foreign Legations in the Chinese capital, Peking, were besieged by the Society of Righteous Harmonious Fists, or Boxers, as they were more commonly known, with support from the Chinese Imperial Army. The British ambassador, Sir Claude MacDonald, managed to send a message through to Admiral

Sir Edward Seymour, whose squadron was moored 120 miles away at Taku at the mouth of the Peiho River.

Seymour had mustered a force of 1,800 sailors and marines from his squadron and took four junks up the Peiho, where they were impeded by a destroyed railway bridge. Taking to the land, Seymour's force retreated through dangerous country towards Tientsin. With over 230 wounded and food running low, they were forced to stop 40 miles short at Hsiku, where they fortuitously found a Chinese arsenal. Unable to force their way to Tientsin, they dug in to await rescue.

The Boxers had control of the city of Tientsin but the 2,400-strong International Settlement garrison held out on the southern outskirts of the city. Incidentally, the barricades erected were constructed from bales of merchandise supervised by a future American president, Herbert Hoover. Communications with Taku had been cut and the defenders were running out of ammunition.

On 20 June, a young English civilian named James Watts, a member of the local Tientsin Volunteer Corps, offered to ride from Tientsin to Taku with a message for more men to come and relieve the town. He knew the country well and was an excellent horseman. He rode his horse, Palo Alto, on which he had won several races. He took an escort of three Cossacks and one spare mount. Leaving at night they were spotted and pursued almost immediately. As they approached the numerous villages, they either galloped through or deviated to avoid the crowds of hostile Chinese. In one village, he was recognised and the mob became menacing. Rather than shoot his way out, he dug in his heels and his horse charged through the crowd. The small group also had to ride over the humpback bridges, another danger point, and there were several narrow escapes. At one point, the four horsemen had to swim the Peiho twice to avoid capture.

Watts had his beloved horse shot from under him and changed onto the spare pony. As they approached the coast, they were helped by the sea mist that rolled in giving them cover. They reached Taku having ridden 40 miles through enemy territory. Watts had been in the saddle for twelve hours but when he arrived he found that the ships had been stripped of the crews who had left with Admiral Seymour. Watts reported to Rear Admiral Bruce, who sent a telegram to the Admiralty:

> Reinforcements most urgently required. Casualties have been heavy. Supplies of ammunition insufficient. Machine-guns or field-guns required. Beware ambush near Tientsin. Russians at railway station hard pressed. Chinese maintain incessant fire with large guns on European Concession (International Settlement), nearly all burnt. There are no reinforcements to send.

Luckily, HMS *Terrible* had just arrived from South Africa and a Russian troopship had arrived from Vladivostok, bringing the numbers to 500 men. In the light of the information delivered by Watts, the reinforcements set off right away. Travelling by rail alongside the Peiho River, they had to contend with burning sleepers blocking the railway and the Boxers setting up ambushes. They reached Hsiku on the 26th, which they relieved having lost 62 dead and 228 wounded. They then went on to the International Settlement at Tientsin, collected the defenders and marched on to Peking.

At the end of this short but fierce war, awards were recommended. Victoria Crosses were bestowed to Captain Lewis Halliday for the defence of the Peking Legations and Midshipman Basil Guy for the relief of Tientsin. Admiral Seymour supported James Watts's ride and he was expected to be awarded the Victoria Cross. The Under Foreign Secretary officially 'regretted' that there was no means of rewarding the conduct of a civilian not in government employment.

It was the allies, namely Germany and Belgium, who were first with the decorations, which led to questions being asked on 2 April 1901 in Parliament. This was followed by a media protest in which the *Pall Mall Gazette* wrote:

> That this country should have to be taught by a foreign sovereign how a British subject ought to be rewarded for an act of distinguished gallantry, is not creditable to us, how ever much it is to the Kaiser. How long is this sort of stupid snobbery – which cannot recognise bravery in a civilian – to be tolerated?

Edward VII found a way of breaking through Foreign Office red tape and suggested awarding the Order of St Michael and St George – a decoration for rewarding diplomats and civil servants. The pressure from the press found its mark, for on 13 May 1901, James Watts received his award.

Chapter 6

Nepotism and Patronage

The new gallantry award greatly excited the officer class, who saw the VC as a step up the promotion ladder. Colin Campbell, in his dour Scottish manner, saw the Victoria Cross 'as quite unnecessary in the British Army'. The Victoria Cross has largely been shielded from the accusations of nepotism but two examples have left a lingering bitter taste while a third example of patronage led to the posthumous award of the Victoria Cross. The most blatant occurred during the First Relief of Lucknow from June to September 1857. Brigadier General Henry Havelock had employed his son, also named Henry but familiarly called Harry, as an aide on his staff in the Persian War and did so again in the current conflict.

Harry was born on 6 August 1830 at Cawnpore. When he was just 15, he was commissioned as Ensign with the 39th (Dorset) Regiment before becoming a lieutenant by purchase with 86th (Royal Ulster) Regiment. He then transferred to the 10th (Lincolnshire) Regiment as Adjutant in 1852 and was appointed to his father's staff for the Persian War and the Indian Mutiny.

Towards the end of the battle at Aherwa, which is more commonly referred to as the First Battle of Cawnpore, Nana Sahib's force had pulled back to a position where they were supported by a 24-pounder. The British attack began to falter as casualties mounted from this well-sited gun. With the 64th and 78th regiments taking cover after their huge efforts in pushing back the enemy, General Havelock called for one last charge to take the 24-pounder, which stood between them and Cawnpore.

Accounts of what happened next differ widely. The 64th was chosen to head the attack, led on foot by their commander, Major Thomas Stirling, whose horse had been shot. Without instructions, Harry Havelock, the General's ADC, also placed himself in the front of the regiment on horseback and at walking pace, headed directly for the enemy's cannon. All the time the regiment was under heavy fire but when they got within range, they charged with the bayonet and soon captured the gun, putting Nana's men to flight.

As the only horseman in the advance, Harry Havelock was provisionally recommended for the Victoria Cross by his father. This was later endorsed by General James Outram, who arrived in Cawnpore on 16 September to take overall command.

Lieutenant Havelock's citation, published in the *London Gazette* on 15 January 1858, reads:

> In the combat at Cawnpore, Lieutenant Havelock was my Aide-de-camp. The 64th Regiment had been under much artillery fire, from which it severely suffered. The whole of the infantry were lying down in line, when, perceiving that the enemy had brought out the last reserved gun, a 24-pounder, and were rallying around it, I called up the regiment to rise and advance. Without another word from me, Lieutenant Havelock placed himself on his horse, in front of the centre of the 64th, opposite the muzzle of the gun. Major Stirling, commanding the regiment, was in front, dismounted, but the Lieutenant continued to move steadily on in front of the regiment at foot pace, on his horse. The gun discharged shot until the troops were within a short distance, when they fired grape. In went the corps, led by the Lieutenant, who still steered steadily on the gun's muzzle until it was mastered by a rush of the 64th.
>
> (Extract of a telegram from the late Major General Sir Henry Havelock to the Commander-in-Chief in India, dated Cawnpore, August 18th, 1857)

The recommendation had bypassed the Commander-in-Chief India and was sent to London via the Governor General and the EIC Court of Directors, which further irked Campbell. Lieutenant Harry Havelock later recalled the battle and his part in it:

> Eager to get ahead of the Highlanders, the 64th had got a little in advance of their front lines when all at once a shrapnel shell from the 24-pounder in their front struck their No. 5 Company, burst, and knocked over six men, one of whom was killed and the other five awfully mutilated. At this, someone shouted out that they were to lie down. They got into confusion. Many broke their ranks and ran back into the village for shelter, and it looked as if they were going to break into a general rout. ... I rode up, dismounted, and got the men out of the village by abuse and entreaties. I then got them to lie down in the front line. There the wounded men were left groaning a few paces in advance of the line; and Major Stirling, the commander, instead of sending a few men to remove them, kept

beckoning and calling out to me, in the presence of his regiment, 'For God's sake, get some help for these poor fellows.'

I at last went over and quietly spoke to him about it, and he left off his whining and the men were removed as I suggested. I had noticed earlier in the day that his nerves were badly shaken, and now the thing was critical enough in itself without his making it worse. And I confess that I thought it was all up with us. …

I must confess that I felt absolutely sick with apprehension; and if I looked calm, I never was before and hope never to be gain in such a funk in my life …

Just then, the General rode bareheaded to the front. He was the only man who dared raise his head, so close and thick was the fire that rained down upon us; but he had a charmed life, and had come out of some thirty actions without a scratch, though he had lost many a mount. He pulled up with his back to the fire; and smiling, he said clearly and calmly, 'The longer you look at it, men, the less you will like it. We must silence those noisy guns. Rise up! The brigade will extend in skirmishing order to the left, in battalion echelon from the left.' I think I was the first on my feet, shouting, 'Get up, men, and take those damned guns!'

I rode on the right flank of the 64th. … However, contrary to the General's wishes and the rules of the Service, these same officers dismounted and were advancing on foot so as to be less exposed. They were hardly visible to their men and consequently lost in the ranks as far as example or leadership was concerned.

Major Stirling later claimed that he was on foot because his pony was rendered unrideable by a shell bursting close by. If this was the same animal he was riding the day before, I can understand its excitability. For I saw it on the loose and advancing on its hind legs, determined to bite some other horse if possible, and I had to draw my sword to defend my own mount if necessary. But it doesn't explain the Major's allowing his subordinates to dismount. And worst of all, he was merely grazed on the left shoulder and immediately went to the rear. I then asked each of the three other senior officers of the regiment to take his place; but they all declined, saying it was not their duty to do so. This was poppycock, of course, and they knew it; but there was no time to argue the matter; so I rode forward at once and led the regiment myself, shaming and ridiculing them into steadiness over those twelve hundred yards of level ground, with the enemy blazing shot and shell into us the whole way. …

To say nothing of the other officers, this action of mine was in itself highly irregular; and I got criticised for it afterwards, especially as I did it without orders; but I had no regrets, considering the irregular conduct of the other officers, and the General thought it was an action worthy of the Victoria Cross; for if it didn't save India, at least it saved the day.

There is little dispute that Harry Havelock performed an act of gallantry, something he was to often repeat. In response to the accusations of nepotism, his father issued a disclaimer stating that:

> On this spontaneous statement of the Major-General [Sir James Outram] the Brigadier General [Havelock] consents to award the Cross to this officer which, if originating from himself, might from the near relationship Lieutenant Havelock bears to him, assume the appearance of undue partiality.

It certainly did reek of nepotism and caused much resentment among other officers, particularly those of the 64th. When the wording of the citation reached India, the officers of the 64th felt that it badly reflected on them and wrote to Sir Colin Campbell, the new Commander-in-Chief. Never an advocate of the Victoria Cross, he sent the officer's letter to the Adjutant General with his own pithy comments:

> This instance is one of many in which, since the institution of the Victoria Cross, advantage has been taken by young Aides-de-Camp and other staff officers to place themselves in prominent positions for the purpose of attracting attention. To them life is of little value, as with the gain of a public honour, but they do not reflect, and the General to whom they belong do not reflect, on the cruel injustice thus done to gallant office, who beside the excitement of the moment in, have all the responsibility attendant on the situation. By such despatches as the one above alluded to, it is made to appear to the world that a regiment would prove wanting in courage, except for an accidental ... such a reflection is most galling to British soldiers, indeed it is almost intolerable, and the fact is remembered against it by all the other corps in Her Majesty's service. Soldiers feel such things very keenly. I would, therefore, again beg leave to dwell on the injustice sometimes done by General officers when they give a public preference to those attached to them over the officers who are charged with the most difficult and responsible duties.

As if rubbing salt into the wounds of the 64th (Staffordshire), Harry Havelock's father recommended that a bar earned in 1858 should be added to his son's Cross. This received short shift from General Campbell, who wrote:

> a bar in 1858 was rejected on the grounds that it was clear that the feelings of the Army in India was that he [Harry] had not won the Cross when conferred on him by his father and, therefore, effectively the original award stood for the second act of gallantry.

Harry Havelock received his Victoria Cross from the Queen on 8 June 1859. He also succeeded to the baronetcy bestowed on his father, who died of dysentery at Lucknow within hours of the Residency being relieved by Campbell's force. Parliament also awarded annual pensions of £1,000 to both Harry and his mother.

At the age of 67, Havelock, now created colonel of his old regiment, the 18th (Royal Irish) Regiment, visited them on the North-West Frontier. They were part of the Malakand expedition under General Sir William Lockhart, who provided an escort for his visitor. On 30 December 1897, promising not to take any unnecessary risks but unable to resist the thrill of danger, Havelock rode on ahead of his escort and was shot dead by Afridi tribesmen. He was later buried at Rawalpindi but the whereabouts of his VC group is unknown.

The second example of nepotism happened during the Anglo-Zulu War. On 28 March 1879, Evelyn Wood, the Colonel of the 90th (Perthshire Volunteers), commanded the Left Flank Column in the northern part of Zululand. After the Battle of Isandlwana, the other two columns retreated to the Natal side of the Buffalo River. Wood's command, based at Kambula inside Zululand, was left to capture the Zulus' cattle, destroy the *kraals* and burn their crops. Wood had misgivings about attacking Hlobane, a Zulu stronghold, although he knew its threat had to be neutralised. Buller, with a mounted force of 400 men, was enthusiastic, not only to defeat the chieftain, Mblini, but also the prospect of capturing so many head of cattle that roamed the plateau and the prize money they brought. Hlobane Mountain was a formidable position to take. It rose 1,500 feet above the surrounding plain, being 3 miles long by about a mile wide. Narrow tracks led up the steep flanks to the summit, which was a moor-like plateau littered with boulders and scrub. It would be hard to find an objective more unsuited for mounted troops. Wood decided not to take any of his infantry, except for his native irregulars, to round up the cattle and drive them back to Kambula.

The debacle that followed left a question mark about Evelyn Wood's state of mind, for he ignored standard military practice and had no control over the fighting. He adopted a 'floating' form of command, which meant he followed at a distance and was quite unable to influence events. It was left to Redvers Buller, in command of the irregular mounted troops, to dictate the fighting.

Wood and his small entourage made their leisurely way along the base of the mountain with the intention of following Buller's route to the summit. Flattened grass, discarded bits of equipment and the odd dead horse made the trail easy to follow. Soon they heard the sound of gunfire echoing from above. Shortly afterwards they came upon the Border Horse riding towards them and claiming that they had lost their way. Wood forcefully persuaded the commander, Colonel Weatherley, to turn about and accompany him to the summit. With Wood and his staff in the lead, they began to climb when a fusillade of shots rang out from some rocks and caves above them.

To Wood's horror, his trusted interpreter and political officer, Llewellyn Lloyd, was struck and mortally wounded. Wood had him carried to a nearby cattle *kraal*, where most of the party had taken cover. Advancing once more, Wood's horse was shot and he was pinned beneath its body. Struggling clear, he instructed his ADC, Captain Ronald Campbell, to order Weatherly's men to flush out the Zulus, but this they refused to do. Calling the men of the Border Horse 'cowards', Campbell, together with another staff man, the 20-year-old Lieutenant Henry Lysons, and Private Edmund Fowler of the escort, charged amongst the rocks and into the entrance of a cave. As Campbell was framed in silhouette, a point-blank shot to his head felled him. Lysons and Fowler stepped over the dead staff man and fired into the recesses of the cave in an attempt to scatter the Zulus.

Wood appeared to have been gripped by shock and guilt. In the space of a few minutes he had seen two of his favourite staff killed for little good reason. Gathering the two corpses, he retreated to the base of the mountain, where he acted out a bizarre ceremony. With a battle raging above him on the summit and part of a large Zulu force from Ulundi in the south fanning out to envelope Hlobane, Wood concentrated on burying his staff men. Instead of leaving the bodies or even tying them to their horses to lead back to camp, Wood insisted that they should be buried on the spot. A sort of blinkered obsession overcame him and all the surrounding dangers were blanked out. He even sent his bugler, Private Walkinshaw, back up the slope, under fire, to retrieve a prayer book from the saddlebag on his dead horse.

It was Wood's insistence to launch a frontal assault on the well-entrenched sharpshooters that led to the deaths of his favourite staff men. Also on his conscience should have been the deaths of six Border troopers who were killed fending off the attacks from the rocks and scrub above. With no digging tools, Wood ordered his Zulu Irregulars to use their *assegais* to dig a grave. Despite its unsuitability as a spade, the *assegais* managed to fashion a hole about 4 feet deep. The two bodies were lowered into their resting place only to find that the grave was too short. Some further frenzied digging allowed the corpses to be laid out straight and the grave to be filled. Accompanied by a background of gunfire, Wood read a short service over the grave.

Giving up ascending the mountain, Wood's small group made their way slowly westward along the base of Hlobane. At this time they were quite unaware that the 20,000-strong *impi* from Ulundi were swiftly advancing to cut them off.

Wood then ordered Henry Lysons to ride to the western end of Hlobane with a message for brevet Lieutenant Colonel John Russell's party to retire to 'Zunguin Nek'. Due to confusion as to its whereabouts, Russell took his men several miles away, adding to the pressure on Colonel Buller's retreating men on Hlobane.

Finally, one of Wood's Zulu scouts spotted the approaching horde and this galvanised Wood into some action. Another account tells quite a different story. Private Fowler, who had charged into the cave with Campbell and Lysons, wrote home in a letter:

> After we had ridden about three miles, we saw on our right front [suggest left front is correct] the whole of the Zulu army. The old man (Wood) says 'Gallop for your lives men' which we did, and a hard run we had of it for twenty-five miles. All the poor chaps that we left behind us were cut off and killed. We had a lucky escape, and when we reached camp (Kambula) and told the news it caused a great sensation.

To his shame, Wood sought to cover up his mistakes by eulogising the deaths of Campbell and Lloyd, both sons of wealthy and influential families. He stated and later wrote on 15 October 1881 from Government House, Pietermaritzburg:

> Without wishing to take away in the slightest degree from the bravery evinced by Lieutenant Lysons and Private Fowler, I should add that if Captain Ronald Campbell had survived, I should have recommended him for the Victoria Cross before the others, as in the assault of such a cave, as I have attempted to describe, the greatest danger is necessarily received by the Leader.

The comments Wood made about awarding Campbell the Victoria Cross had he survived was picked up by General Sir Daniel Lysons, the Quartermaster General in the War Office. He was known as 'Wily Dan' for his machinations and his main object was to obtain a VC for his son. Being in the War Office, he was in frequent contact with the Commander-in-Chief, the Duke of Cambridge and raised the question of his son's valour at Hlobane. In a letter he wrote to his son, he stated that he should have been awarded the Cross as Captain Campbell had been killed but recommended for the same act. In fact, the deaths and injuries in the flurry of shooting by the Zulus had died down and Campbell's death was the last shot as the Zulus escaped into the subterranean maze.

When Wood returned from South Africa, General Lysons lobbied and pressurised him until it finally paid off. In 1881, the warrant was altered to include acts of bravery performed in the course of duty. This let Wood off the hook and he wrote to the Duke of Cambridge's military secretary, enclosing letters from Sir Daniel and Lady Lysons. He added that he wished to recommend both Henry Lysons and Edmund Fowler for the Victoria Cross. He further stated that Lady Lysons had said that her son ought to have been recommended for the Victoria Cross and now, with the new warrant, he would like to do so. He also felt he should put Private Fowler's name forward as he was in the forefront of the advance to the cave. On 5 April 1882, the Queen gave her permission to confer the Victoria Crosses on Lysons and Fowler three years after the ambush; a very strange conclusion to what had been a minor event. In fact, all Lysons and Fowler did was to fire into an empty cave – hardly a VC act. The final act was a pencilled note regarding a similar recommendation to Captain Ronald Campbell had he survived. It simply said 'Gen. W. [Wolseley] does not wish this question to be raised'. And nothing came of it.

The following day, the Zulu army attacked the camp at Kambula, where Henry Lysons displayed his bravery in helping to rescue a wounded soldier who had fallen before the advancing warriors. The well-entrenched British fired volley after volley to be followed up by the mounted men pursuing the Zulus for miles. The British lost 29 killed and 54 wounded. The Zulu figure is unknown, ranging from 1,000 to 2,000 killed. The effect on the morale of the Zulu warriors at Kambula was severe and contributed to the final defeat of the Zulu nation at Ulundi.

Redvers Buller was described by Archibald Forbes, the war correspondent, as 'a stern-tempered, ruthless, saturnine man, with a gift of grim silence'. Certainly he was very brave and was one of the few men to be awarded the Victoria Cross for exceptional gallantry during the Zulu War. He should have remained as a colonel but, as a man of action, he was promoted to general. By the end of the century he had lost his energetic wiry appearance and become overweight and ponderous. In 1899, somewhat to his surprise, Buller was selected to be Commander-in-Chief in South Africa in the event of a war. With reluctance, he was persuaded to accept and, in doing so, ruined his high reputation.

Buller's campaign to relieve Ladysmith was littered with humiliating defeats and costly victories, none worse than the 15 December 1899 battle at Colenso. It was here that Colonel Long, Buller's chief of artillery, brought his guns so close to the Boer positions that his gunners were swept away by rifle fire, leaving the guns standing exposed and unmanned. Akin to the infantry losing their regimental colour, any suggestion that the twelve guns should be left by the Artillery was unthinkable. General Buller called for volunteers to ride forward to retrieve the guns.

One who immediately volunteered was Freddie Roberts, the only son of Field Marshal Lord Roberts of Kandahar. Lieutenant Roberts was travelling to join the King's Royal Rifle Corps, but found it was one of the regiments trapped inside Ladysmith. Instead, he was employed as an ADC and galloper by Lieutenant General Sir Francis Clery, commander of the 2nd Infantry Division. According to Thomas Pakenham in *The Boer War*, 'Freddie Roberts was a delightful fellow; but not very bright, unfortunately; that summer he had failed the Staff College entrance examination by a record margin.' It took his father's influence for him to pass his exams and be admitted.

Along with Captains Harry Schofield and Walter Congreve, Freddie galloped off to the *donga* in front of them where the gun teams and ammunition wagons were sheltering. They assembled two teams of six horses each and made the 500-yard gallop to the deserted guns. This dash probably caught the Boers by surprise since the teams made it to the guns. A stray bullet hit Freddie Roberts in the groin, and this proved fatal. The survivors managed to take cover in a shallow *donga*, in which they stayed under a sweltering sun for the rest of the day.

General Buller was stricken with guilt having sent Lord Roberts's only son forward to face the Boer fire. In order to alleviate the shock of Freddie's death on the Roberts family, he decided to award the VC to the young man, who had done little more than ride with the group towards the abandoned guns. On the morning of the 17th, Freddie Roberts succumbed to his wound. According to Captain Schofield's account, the VC was awarded by Buller, who gave it to him just before he died. The Seventh Section of the warrant allows the award to be conferred on the spot when the 'act has been performed is under the eye and command of an Admiral or General Officer commanding the Forces'. Buller was General Officer Commanding (GOC) and so his award would have been binding. Until the award to Freddie Roberts, those who paid the ultimate price while carrying out a commendably brave deed carried the citation 'would have been awarded the Victoria Cross if they had survived'. This citation ceased in 1902 with the recognition of the award to nine applicants, and no further retrospective claims were accepted.

Buller made the award under his authority while Freddie was still alive. One can imagine the reaction of the Awards Committee at the War Office in Whitehall, who had been applying the rule that if the deed results in the death of the 'doer' and his name would have appeared in the *London Gazette*. The recommendation for the award naturally passed through the statutory approvals procedure for ratification and it thus eventually arrived in front of the Queen herself. By this stage, poor Freddie had died, and there is no doubt that the normal processes of sanctioning the award would have said that his death had made him ineligible for the VC. A combination of the death of the only son of Britain's greatest Victorian hero, the swift recommendation for the VC made by the commander who sent Freddie to his death and the lavish awarding of seven Crosses for what was a foolish error of judgement was acceptable to the public, and Freddie Roberts became the first posthumous recipient of the VC.

In a despatch from Chieveley on 16 December 1899, Buller made recommendations for mentioned in despatches and medals. He was lavish in his praise and awards for bravery but he turned down one man. He wrote:

> I have differentiated in my recommendations, because I thought that a recommendation for the Victoria Cross required proof of initiative, something more, in fact, than mere obedience to orders, and for this reason I have not recommended Captain Schofield, RA, who was acting under orders, though I desire to record his conduct as most gallant.

Oddly enough, Buller recommended the Victoria Cross to men who failed to retrieve a gun but gave the lesser award of the DCM to the men who brought back two guns. Captain Harry Schofield, Buller's aide, was to receive the DSO. In April 1901, a re-evaluation of the Colenso VCs under General Lord Roberts strongly felt that Harry Schofield should receive the Victoria Cross instead of the DSO. This was changed when he relinquished his DSO, held for just thirty days, and he was rewarded with the Victoria Cross. Supported by Captain Congreve, Lord Roberts wrote to the Secretary of State for War:

> I think that Pte Ravenhill (Released as a POW) and Captain Schofield should both get the VC for their actions in endeavouring to save the guns at Colenso. I was reading Sir Redvers Buller's dispatch again the other day and intend to bring Major Schofield's conduct to your notice.

Harry Schofield, now promoted to major, received his Victoria Cross on 29 October 1901 from King Edward VII at Buckingham Palace.

Chapter 7

Old Practices and Bending the Rules

Another example of excessive awarding of the Victoria Cross was the attack on 21 August 1860 on the North Taku Fort during the Third China War. Six Victoria Crosses were given, mainly to men who were 'first in' to the fort. General Sir James Hope Grant recommended these officers and men from the 44th and 67th Regiments but was denied by the War Office. Grant responded by writing:

> To two of these, Ensign Chaplin and Private Lane, I made a promise at the time that I would recommend them for this distinction and in doing so I did not avail myself of the power conferred by that clause of the Royal Warrant which allows the Commander of the Forces to confer the Victoria Cross on the spot for actions performed under his observation, and which power so given was almost tantamount to a provisional bestowal of that distinction.

Ensign John Chaplin of the 67th (Hampshire) was carrying the Queen's colour and planted it with the assistance of Private Thomas Lane on the breach made by the storming party. He then went on to plant the colours on the bastion of the fort and was severely wounded.

A repeat performance by a young ensign followed in 1868 with a rescue force sent to Abyssinia. King Theodore, the Abyssinian monarch, had imprisoned some forty Europeans, mostly missionaries and artisans, for over five years. After years of discussion, it was finally decided to mount a rescue expedition. General Sir Robert Napier, who had been an engineer with the Bengal Army, was placed in command. Napier, now Commander-in-Chief of the Bombay Presidency Army, was the best man that could have been chosen for such a task.

His planning, organisation and attention to the support he put in place was probably the best run expedition of the Victorian era.

Setting out from their anchorage at Annesley Bay on the Red Sea, General Napier's force marched 390 miles inland to the mountaintop fortress of King Theodore. One of the regiments in Napier's force was the 33rd (Duke of Wellington), largely made up of Irishmen, whom H.L. Stanley described as 'hard drinkers all'. They were commanded by Colonel Alexander Dunn, the only VC officer in the Charge of the Light Brigade. He was described by one of his youngest officers, Ensign Walter Wynter, rather disparagingly as: 'A tall handsome man, 30 years of age ... a kind, good-natured dandy, a bad Commanding Officer and not a good example to young officers – he was very popular but nearly destroyed the regiment.'

Sadly, Dunn was killed in a hunting accident while shooting duck at Senafe near the start of the Abyssinian campaign.

The brief battle at the foot of Magdala, in which the natives were thoroughly defeated, meant that the fortress had to be taken. The infantry assault started on 13 April about 4.00 pm. The steep climb brought the 33rd to the gates of the fortress. Giving covering fire, the Royal Engineers went forward to blow the gates. On reaching the entrance it was discovered that both scaling ladders and powder bags had been left behind and the gate could not be forced. The commander, General Staveley, was furious and ordered the 33rd to find an alternative way in. On each side of the gate the walls were protected by a thorn hedge that led to another gate. After ascending the cliff face, Private Begin found a gap and Drummer Michael Magner climbed on his shoulders and reached the top of the wall. He then pulled Begin up beside him and together they began firing.

The 33rd had taken their colours into action carried by Ensign Walter Wynter. He was hauled up and over the wall. There was a great rush to get him forward so the colour was seen by General Staveley. Ensign Wynter recalled:

> I was hardly ever on my feet, as the men took me and the Colour in their arms and passed me from the centre to the front of the column. I shall never forget the exhilaration of that moment, the men firing and shouting like madmen.

He was soon in position and waving the colour frantically to the accompaniment of a great outburst of cheering from below. A party went to the main gate and managed to open it and the remainder of the 33rd poured through. There was very little resistance as the occupants retreated. King Theodore was seen to dodge behind a pile of hay and was chased. The soldiers found that he had committed suicide using a silver-mounted pistol sent to him by Queen Victoria.

Casualties were light on the British side: just two killed and eighteen wounded. It was estimated that 700 Abyssinians had been killed and 1,200 wounded. Ensign Wynter's flag waving was not recognised as worthy of a gallantry award. In fact, this custom was considered outdated and in 1881, it was discontinued. The last VC awarded for carrying the colours was to Midshipman Duncan Boyes for the 1864 action during the Shimonoseki campaign in Japan.

After the flurry of Victoria Crosses being awarded for the Crimean and Indian wars, there was a hiatus of about fifteen years before a number of VCs were again awarded. During the Ashanti War of 1873–74, four Victoria Crosses were awarded, one of which caused the Awards Committee some problem.

Reginald William Sartorius was a major in the 6th Bengal Cavalry and when war was declared against the belligerent Ashanti tribe in the Gold Coast, like many officers, he applied to be part of this expedition in order to come to the attention of the High Command. He took leave in 1873 and was attached as a special service officer in the Ashanti campaign.

He was sent to Accra to serve with the nascent Gold Coast Constabulary, made up of the Hausa, a largely Muslim group recruited from Nigeria. They were commanded by Captain John Glover RN, who had been appointed administrator and colonial secretary of Lagos Colony until 1872. In September 1873, he marched from Cape Coast to Accra and built up a considerable force of local natives who had a strong hatred of the Ashantis. Unfortunately, this hatred disappeared when it came to confronting their formidable enemy, so Glover had to rely on his well-trained Hausas to take on the Ashantis.

On 16 January 1874, Glover's 3,000-strong force crossed the Volta River and made its first advance into Ashanti territory from the east. The first fight was at the village of Abugu (Abogu), which was taken at a rush. In a stiff fight, Glover lost three men killed and several wounded. Separated by miles of jungle, communication with Wolseley's column, approaching from the coast, was virtually impossible. Guessing that Wolseley had reached Kumasi some 45 miles away, Glover pressed on deeper into Ashanti territory and captured Konomo after another fierce fight.

Glover was forced to pause and wait for the ammunition supply to catch up but was loath to delay the chance of meeting up with Wolseley's column. By now they were only 25 miles from Kumasi, a distance that could be accomplished by a few men in a forced march.

Contact with the main column was essential and Glover chose Captain Sartorius and 130 men to make this dangerous journey. Very soon Sartorius found he had been completely cut off from Glover. Deciding to minimise his force even further to speed up his advance on Kumasi, Sartorius sent forty of his force back to Glover. Coming upon two villages, Sartorius's small unit fought their way through with just one man injured.

With his flank being menaced by Glover, the Ashanti king had detached part of his army to confront the eastern column. Unknown to Glover, King Kofi had accepted some of the British demands. Sartorius paused about 6 miles from Kumasi and waited for Glover. When Glover arrived he sent Sartorius with twenty Hausas to deliver a letter to Wolseley at Kumasi asking for orders and to return the next day.

Glover became alarmed when Sartorius did not return the following day and ordered the column forward to Kumasi. When he entered, he found the place partially burned and deserted. Wolseley had already departed. Glover decided to follow Wolseley's trail and catch up with him. Soon he came upon a white man who had been decapitated and he feared it was Sartorius. Nearby, he found one of his wounded Hausas propped under a tree with provisions left by Sartorius two days previous. It became apparent that Sartorius's small band had passed through Kumasi two days before and after a perilous 35-mile journey through territory teeming with Ashanti, reached Wolseley on 12 February. Later, Glover recalled Sartorius's endurance and leadership in leading his small band through enemy jungle:

> They heard the rustling of invisible movement in the bush dogging them all the way; in the evening the enemy openly menaced them, and they had to halt in a slightly defensible position, and nothing by Sartorius's personal forwardness induced the Hausas to move in the morning.

Sartorius finally caught up with Wolseley's camp just outside Kumasi just as King Kofi accepted terms. Wolseley was full of praise for Sartorius's feat: 'A most remarkable march of 53 miles through the heart of the enemy's country, often surrounded or threatened, without provisions, and without having fired a single shot or lost a man of his small escort.'

A VC was suggested and was brought to the attention of the War Office on 11 July 1874. Although Wolseley and the colonial secretary, Lord Carnarvon, were keen for Sartorius to receive the Cross, his perilous trek did not seem to be covered by the terms of the warrant. Also, as the only white man in the command there was no one to give adequate testimony as to his conduct. The Duke of Cambridge suggested that the citation should also cover the ride to Kumasi as it was apparent that it was this perilous journey that had really earned the decoration. The Secretary of State for War ruled, however, that it could only be recommended for a specific individual act. After much thought and exchanges of correspondence, a solution was found. In the first confrontation with the Ashanti at the village of Abugo on 17 January, and under the command of Captain Glover, Reginald Sartorius performed an act of bravery. This was reflected in the citation that appeared in the *London Gazette* dated 27 October 1874:

> For having during the attack on Abogoo, on 17th January last, removed under a heavy fire Sergeant Major Braimah Doctor, a Hausa Non-Commissioned Officer, who was mortally wounded, and placed him under cover.

This bending of the rules satisfied the civil servants although Sartorius never believed his award was for his deed at Abugo but for his journey through the jungles of the Ashanti. On 30 March 1875, Reginald Sartorius was invested with his Victoria Cross by Queen Victoria at Windsor. His brother, Euston Henry, joined him six years later as a VC recipient during the Afghan War.

Hans Garrett Moore was the son of an officer in the 88th (Connaught Rangers). He followed his father into the regiment and was commissioned. With the outbreak of the Indian Mutiny, his regiment joined General Rose's Central Column where he displayed his undoubted appetite for fighting. One such was the storming of the fortified village of Birwah on 21 October, which resulted in the 88th's largest list of casualties. The fight lasted eight hours, with the 88th bearing the brunt of the fighting. Moore was again in the thick of the battle, during which his revolver was broken at his side and 'eights' shot off his cap. Armed only with his sword, he later entered a house and killed three sepoys. His conduct was noted and he was mentioned in despatches.

He ended the campaign with a reputation of being a fearless officer and a tough campaigner. Later, he showed another side to his character when, on a shooting expedition in Oudh, he dived fully clothed into the fast-flowing Gumti River to save a native beater who had fallen in. Moore was a strong swimmer and superb horseman, winning many steeplechases. He also became master of the Connaught Ranger's pack of hounds during their long posting in India.

On 19 June 1872, Garry was promoted to captain but, tiring of being garrisoned in Gosport, applied to join Major General Sir Garnet

Wolseley's expedition to punish the Ashanti tribe, who had invaded the British possessions of Cape Coast. Moore, along with many other ambitious middle ranking officers, saw this as an opportunity 'to be seen' while on campaign. Wolseley was limited to the selection of thirty-six staff and special service officers. In making his choice from among the many volunteers, he looked for thinking soldiers with proven courage. It was little surprise that he included in his selection fellow Irishman Captain Hans Garrett Moore, who joined that elite band of officers nicknamed the 'Ashanti Club'.

The Government's first intention was to raise local native volunteers, but this was always an over-optimistic hope. Eventually Wolseley got his way and three battalions of British soldiers were sent out to march on the Ashanti capital and defeat the enemy in a short-lived campaign. On the successful completion of this short punitive expedition, Moore was rewarded with a Brevet Majority.

The next overseas posting for the 88th was to South Africa, where they arrived in July 1877. Almost immediately they were sent further up the coast to the Transkei in Eastern Cape, where another of the Frontier Wars had erupted. The local colonial troops were too few in number and not well regarded by the British authorities, including the Commander of Imperial Forces, General Sir Arthur Cunynghame. The 88th arrived in East London on 28 August and a detachment commanded by Garry Moore was sent first to Fort Cunynghame and then to Komgha, the seat of the unrest.

On 29 December, mail riders carrying post to the Kei Road Station had been fired on and forced to return to Komgha. The Gaikas now commanded several miles of the road between King William's Town and Komgha and Major Moore was ordered to take thirty-two men of the Frontier Armed and Mounted Police (FAMP) to ride to Draaibosch, the scene of the attack, and investigate.

After some skirmishes with the enemy, the patrol arrived at the burning remains of the Draaibosch Hotel, where they were confronted by about 300 Gaikas. Four police scouts were just ahead of the main body and Moore ordered them to fall back. Dismounted, the scouts fired a few shots before remounting to retire. One of the scouts, Private Giese, was unable to mount his panicked horse and was in immediate danger of being overwhelmed. Seeing this, Garry Moore spurred his horse forward and joined the other three scouts in riding to the stricken policeman's rescue. Fighting his way through the mob of spear-wielding natives, Moore reached Giese too late to save him. The latter had been repeatedly stabbed. Now Moore fought to extricate himself

71

from the clutching hands and was hit by a thrown *assegai*, which stuck in his upper arm.

Reaching the rest of the patrol, he ordered them in to cover but the Gaikas retreated. Moore then calmly sat on a tree stump, smoking his pipe, while the patrol's doctor extricated the *assegai* blade. When the doctor attempted to cut away the sleeve of his patrol jacket, Moore objected, saying, 'Hold on, this is my only coat. Rip it up the seam.'

As the soul Imperial officer present, Moore's version of events was the only report sent forward to General Cunynghame. It would seem that an award of a Victoria Cross may have been mentioned for, some seventeen months later, Moore wrote to Cunynghame again to press his case for the award. He stated that he had been quite alone with Giese when the latter died, and had killed two natives. Also, he and his horse had had been wounded by *assegais* and it was only then that the other three police came up. There is little doubt that Moore wrote his own citation and his appeal to Cunynghame resulted in a quick response. Just six weeks later, the *London Gazette* of 27 June 1879 announced:

> Hans Garret Moore, 88th Foot. For his gallant conduct in risking his own life in endeavouring to save the life of Private Giese of the Frontier Armed Mounted Police, on the occasion of the action with the Gaikas, near Kohgha on the 29 December 1877. It is reported that when a small body of Mounted Police were forced to retire before overwhelming numbers of the enemy, Major Moore observed Private Giese was unable to mount his horse, and was thereby left at the mercy of the Kaffirs. Perceiving the man's danger, Major Moore rode back alone into the midst of the enemy and did not desist in his endeavour to save the man until the latter was killed. Major Moore having shot two Kaffirs and received an assegai wound in the arm during his gallant attempt.

This version of what happened certainly did not square with the members of the FAMP. The scouts who were nearest to Private Giese were Sergeant Dan Harber, Corporal John Court and Private Martindale. Major Moore joined them as they tried to save Giese. Private Martindale's horse was shot from under him and he was rescued by Sergeant Harber, who carried him to safety. As a result of their action, both Harber and Court were promoted. Another disgruntled policeman stated, 'I could not recall the particular deed of heroism that he (Moore) had performed for which he himself recommended that he should be adorned with the VC.'

By the time of the announcement of Moore's VC, the Anglo-Zulu War had been fought amongst great controversy. One of the bones of contention was the dismissive attitude of the British authorities, in particular the Army officers, towards the colonial volunteers. Belatedly, efforts were made to smooth the ruffled colonial feathers and the awarding of the Victoria Cross was extended to include non-Imperial personnel.

As for Garry Moore, there was no suggestion that he was anything but extremely brave, as witnessed by what happened the day after his VC exploit. Despite his painful wound, Moore led a force of thirty FAMP and fifty men of the 88th out from Komgha to Draaibosch. Lining his small force along the crest of a hill overlooking the burnt-out Draaibosch Hotel, Moore faced the advancing Gaikas, who numbered 1,000, with 600 on horseback. Twelve years later, an eye-witness account was published in *The Times*:

> Suddenly, and when they were within about 350 yards of us, they deployed, one half sweeping round our left flank, and the remainder to our right, whilst the horse went at a canter to our rear … the force of the enemy flanking our position in that direction were nearest, and were then charging up the hill with loud cries. Before the movement could be completed the enemy were upon us – some of the FAM Police flung themselves on their horses and rode hard away (I may here mention that others of that force remained and did gallant service afterwards), and the young soldiers of the Rangers, mere boys for the most part, showed no sign of wavering. What at this moment was Colonel Moore doing? He was sitting immovably, calm, on his horse, facing the hordes of the enemy, and issuing the words of command to his forces as if he had been on parade.

Although the firing of his young soldiers was wayward, Moore maintained order and put on such a brave front that the Gaikas did not take advantage of their numerical superiority and retreated after about ninety minutes. The casualties were light: two men killed and three wounded. Garry Moore's horse was hit three times and died the following day. The narrow victory did little to improve relations between the Imperial and colonial participants. The latter resented being made scapegoats by Moore and even suggested that it was the soldiers who had wavered.

Moore was mentioned in despatches and promoted to brevet colonel. On 6 June 1878, he was placed on half pay and the following day took up a new appointment. In the reorganisation that came with the end of the Ninth Frontier War, the FAMP were reorganised into a regular unit of mounted riflemen and designated the Cape Mounted Rifles. Somewhat surprisingly, Garry Moore was appointed their first commanding officer. It is not clear whether this was a popular appointment for both parties but, after just over six months, Moore resigned and returned to England. He ended his army career as lieutenant colonel of the Second Battalion 93rd Highlanders.

Another case of 'bending the regulations' involved one of the great Victorian heroes, Walter Richard Pollock Hamilton. Another Irishman, Hamilton was the nephew of General Sir George Pollock, who led the Army of Retribution after the disastrous retreat in the First Afghan War of 1842. He was commissioned in the 70th (Surrey) Regiment in 1874 before transferring in India to the elite Queen's Own Corps of Guides. Under the command of Captain Wigram Battye, the Guides were accompanied by Captain Pierre Louis Napoleon Cavagnari of the Bengal Staff Corps in one of the many expeditions against the tribes in North West India. Cavagnari was to play a large part in Hamilton's short life.

On 2 April 1879, General Sam Browne learned of a large gathering of tribesmen some miles south-west of Jalalabad. He despatched three columns under Brigadier General Charles Gough VC, which included the Guides Cavalry. On 2 April, Gough's 1,200 men were confronted by 5,000 tribesmen drawn up behind strong stone works. Their flanks were protected by steep bluffs and from their position the ground sloped down towards Gough's position. There seemed no alternative but to attack head-on. Gough sent forward his cavalry and guns to within a mile of the enemy with orders to fire a few rounds before retiring. He hoped to lure the tribesmen out of their position, giving his cavalry and infantry a chance to get at them. The trick worked.

The tribesmen rushed forward to pursue the retiring cavalry and guns. As they broke ranks, they were charged in the right flank by the hidden infantry. In the fierce hand-to-hand struggle the tribesmen were slowly pushed back. At this point, the cavalry were released on the enemy's left flank and shattered it. Early on in the mêlée, Captain Battye was shot in the hip and was forced to walk his horse as the rest of the cavalry charged on. A little while later, he was shot again in the chest and killed. The command devolved on Walter Hamilton who, cheering his men on to avenge his beloved commander's death, reached the enemy line. Here they were confronted with a 9-foot deep *nullah* just in front of them but the Guides were going too fast to avoid it. They plunged down the steep drop and up towards the tribesmen firing at them from the top of the other bank. The enemy were unnerved and fell back as Hamilton and his screaming *sowars* stormed up the slope and cut through them. Hamilton spotted Sowar Dowlut Ram pinned helpless under his dead horse and in immediate danger of being hacked to pieces by three of the enemy. Spurring his horse forward, Hamilton cut down all three assailants and helped extricate the trapped man.

The rest of Gough's force soon arrived and the guns opened fire on the fleeing enemy. Their losses were estimated at 400 dead, while the British lost six dead and forty wounded. Gough's victory was emphatic and he recognised the decisive part played by the Guides Cavalry and their young leader, Lieutenant Hamilton, who he recommended for the Victoria Cross. On 15 May, the Government of India forwarded this recommendation to the India Office in London who, in turn, forwarded it to Horse Guards on 22 July. A further delay followed while the Duke of Cambridge considered the claim. To the disappointment of the India Office, they were informed that Hamilton's act did not come within the regulations of the VC and was, therefore, declined.

Meanwhile, the Treaty of Gandamak was signed between the new Amir, Yakub Khan, and the British, which brought the Second Afghan War to a close – or so it seemed. Part of the agreement was that a British envoy should be resident in Kabul and the British forces withdraw but keep control of the strategic passes on the Frontier. The envoy appointed was Major Cavagnari, who was allowed to bring a small escort with him. To fill this role, he selected Lieutenant Walter Hamilton with twenty-five Guides Cavalry and fifty-two Guides Infantry. The numbers had been kept small for Cavagnari believed that a large escort would inflame Afghan resentment.

They arrived in Kabul on 24 July 1879 and were given quarters in the Bala Hissar fortress. It was a compound containing a cluster of bungalows and huts situated only 250 yards from the Amir's own residence. From the start, the atmosphere was tense. Cavagnari put on an outward show of confidence but was well aware of the surrounding hostility. The Afghans saw him as a symbol of their national humiliation and it was only a matter of time before a spark would set off the powder keg.

This came in the form of members of the Afghan Army, who had been stationed at Herat in the west of the country and had not been involved in the recent fighting. They had not been paid for months and had arrived in Kabul demanding their arrears. They also turned their discontent on the small British presence and demanded to know why they had been allowed to remain in Kabul. A partial payment of their arrears pacified them temporarily and they returned to their cantonment. With all the self-confidence of inexperience, the Herat soldiers started going about the city with drawn swords and inciting the population against the Amir and the British.

Early on the morning of 3 September, the Herat troops again marched on the Bala Hissar demanding the remainder of their back pay. They rejected a further partial payment and decided to go to Cavagnari at the Residency and demand payment from him. This he firmly rejected, resulting in some stone throwing and an attempt at looting. After one of the Guides was fatally struck by a rock, Hamilton's escort fired a few shots over the heads of the rioters. This was a signal for the Afghans to rush off and arm themselves. Cavagnari sent an urgent message to the nearby Amir asking for protection, but there was to be no response.

Within an hour the Afghan soldiers returned fully armed and were joined by a citizen mob. The Residency was wholly unsuitable for defence, being surrounded on three sides by buildings from which the Afghans could pour in a constant fire, causing casualties and forcing Hamilton to pull back his men to the main building. By mid-afternoon, two cannon were brought up and Hamilton led charges against the gun crews but, without the means to spike them, these forays were futile. Two more attempts were made to capture the guns and pull them into the Residency, but the effort of pulling them and defending themselves was too much for the Guides. Finally, the Residency was set on fire and the survivors retreated and prepared to make a last stand. One of the guns blew down a wall behind which a wounded Cavagnari was being tended by Dr Kelly. The mob swarmed through the breach, butchering the two men to death. Hamilton either made one last attempt to silence the gun or decided to take as many of the attackers as he could with him. Leading a few Guides, he charged amongst the enemy, shooting three with his revolver and cutting down two more with his sword. Finally, he was overwhelmed and hacked to death.

The twelve remaining *sowars* were offered the chance to surrender, which they rejected and continued fighting until all were killed. This ended the unequal fight, which came to represent all that was both gallant and noble about the Victorian officer in the face of overwhelming odds. The defence had lasted twelve hours and an estimated 600 Afghans lay dead around the Residency. All the defenders were dead except for seven members of the escort, who were spared. This epic resistance was later recognised with the whole native escort being awarded the Indian Order of Merit and the Corps of Guides was authorised to wear the battle honour 'Residency, Kabul' on its colours and appointments.

Hamilton's death put the Horse Guards in something of a quandary. Having had the recommendation for a VC turned down, the India Office made another approach, pointing out that Hamilton's action was very similar to those of Captain John Cook and Lieutenant

Reginald Hart, both of whom had received Crosses. The Duke of Cambridge was persuaded and agreed that Hamilton's action merited the VC. Unfortunately, this acceptance was dated 16 September and Hamilton had been killed on the 3rd. As there was no provision to grant a VC to anyone who had died before a submission was put before the Queen, Hamilton should have been disqualified.

With the story of the Residency defence in every newspaper and the lionising of young Walter Hamilton, it was decided to bend the rules. In Michael Crook's book *The Evolution of the Victoria Cross*, he refers to a note accompanying the submission to the Queen that had been predated 1 September, two days before Hamilton's death, 'so as to avoid creating an awkward precedent in giving the decoration after death'. The award was announced in the *London Gazette* on 7 October and the Cross sent to Hamilton's father on 25 October.

Chapter 8

Anglo-Zulu War 1879

Of all the Victorian campaigns, the Zulu War has to be the most overhyped yet most fascinating of all. Even people who know little about military history have heard about Rorke's Drift and the film *Zulu*. It was a war that was started in South Africa by local politicians and the military without the approval of the British Government and ended with the dismemberment of the Zulu nation.

This six-month-long campaign produced seventeen Victoria Crosses, not counting an additional two when Lieutenants Nevill Coghill and Teignmouth Melvill were awarded posthumous VCs in 1907. On 22 January 1879, two battles took place just 12 miles apart: the battles of Isandlwana, in which some 1,300 men were killed, and Rorke's Drift, where fifteen were killed and two mortally wounded. One soldier received the Victoria Cross for his rescue of a comrade in the retreat from Isandlwana, while eleven men received the Cross for their defence of Rorke's Drift.

Probably the most deserving of the Rorke's Drift VCs were the men who were positioned in the hospital, converted from the house of Otto Witt, the Swedish pastor. The hospital was on the western extremity of the defence, about 25 yards from the Biscuit Box barrier. Within the confines of this small bungalow, they had knocked loopholes in the outside walls. The Reverend George Smith recalled:

> Private Joseph Williams fired from a small window at the far end of the hospital. Next morning, fourteen warriors were found dead beneath it, besides others along his line of fire. When their ammunition was expended, he and his companions kept the door with their bayonets, but an entrance was subsequently forced and he, poor fellow was seized by the hands, dragged out and killed before the eyes of the others.

Private John Williams and patient Private Billy Horrigan were Joseph Williams's companions who held the Zulus at bay for an hour. John Williams took a pick and began knocking a hole in the wall to drag out the patients. About the same time, Henry Hook, another defender, broke through into their tiny room. Enlarging the hole so they could to pull the patients through, they relied on Joseph Williams as he fired off his last cartridge. He then blocked the door as he desperately wielded his bayonet to defend the helpless patients. John Williams managed to drag three of the patients through the small hole into the temporary safety of the next room. By this time, the thatch had caught fire and the rooms began to fill with smoke. John Williams poked his head back through the hole in time to see Joseph Williams grabbed by the Zulus, stabbed repeatedly and his stomach ripped open. Hook heard John Williams exclaim, 'The Zulus are swarming all over the place. They've dragged Joseph Williams out and killed him.'

The five surviving defenders, Henry Hook, John Williams, William Allen, Robert Jones and William Jones, managed to delay the Zulus by knocking holes in the partition walls and get nine patients to safety. Joseph Williams had done as much as his fellow soldiers, but there was no retrospective VC for him. His only memorial is at Rorke's Drift but he is mentioned in the citations of John Williams and Henry Hook. Had Joseph Williams survived, he would have received the Victoria Cross for his exceptional gallantry.

The distribution of the Victoria Crosses to the defenders of Rorke's Drift has always been contentious. The original recommendations were correct in every way. Lieutenant Gonville Bromhead submitted to his commander, Colonel Glyn, the names of B Company men who had performed gallant feats during the defence: Corporal William Allen, Privates Henry Hook, John Williams, William Jones and Robert Jones, with Frederick Hitch as being prominent on the barricade.

Glyn passed these names to the General Lord Chelmsford, who, in an effort to diminish the disaster of Isandlwana, added the names of Lieutenants John Chard and Gonville Bromhead. Without referring the matter to Colonel Glyn, who was in a state of shock at the loss of his regiment, two of the Army's less dynamic officers were elevated to recipients of the Victoria Cross. Bromhead suffered from incipient deafness, making him introspective and non-communicative, while Chard was regarded as slow and lazy.

Lieutenant Colonel Arthur Pickard VC, an equerry to Queen Victoria, wrote to Sir Evelyn Wood after John Chard had been summoned to Balmoral to meet the Queen:

> It seemed odd to me that he was not consulted on the distribution of the VCs. But it is only one of the things that 'no fellow can understand'. He is not a genius, and not quick, but a quiet plodding, dogged sort of fellow who will hold his own in most situations in which, as an English officer, his lot may be cast.

Lieutenant General Garnet Wolseley, who replaced Lord Chelmsford as Commander-in-Chief, was more forthcoming when he stated:

> It is monstrous making heroes of those who saved or attempted to save their lives by bolting or of those who, shut up in buildings at Rorke's Drift, could not bolt, and fought like rats for their lives which they could not otherwise save.

This generous awarding of the VC prompted other political and military establishments to lobby their own men. The Army Medical Department felt that Surgeon James Reynolds should be included among those honoured as he had patched up the wounded in a makeshift redoubt in front of the storehouse. He had also handed ammunition to those inside the hospital and received a bullet that passed through his helmet. He did rather well as he leapfrogged those above him to be promoted to surgeon major. Together with John Chard, Reynolds received his Cross from General Wolseley on 16 July 1879 at St Paul's Mission en route to Ulundi. The Medical Council further voted that Reynolds should receive the Gold Medal for Distinguished Merit, the highest award in the medical profession.

Of all the military men trapped inside Rorke's Drift, the one with the most experience and who insisted they stay and make a defence was Acting Assistant Commissary James Dalton. He knew they had just the right sort of stores to erect breastworks: heavy sacks of grain, boxes of biscuit, barrels of lime juice and ox wagons. Chard later reported that Dalton's 'energy, intelligence and gallantry were of the greatest service to us'. Supervised by Chard, Bromhead and Dalton, a solid barricade was erected encompassing the hospital and storehouse, which were about 40 yards apart. Dalton was also active at the barricades until he was wounded. He was carried to the mealie sack redoubt and placed inside, his role in the battle effectively over. It was his decision to stay and fight rather than risk a slow-moving column caught in the open, which saved many lives.

The Commissary General, Sir Edward Strickland, orchestrated a campaign for both Dalton and Assistant Commissary Walter Dunne to be recognised and received a letter of support from John Chard. When the appeal finally reached the Duke of Cambridge, the Commander-in-Chief rejected Dunne's claim and commented, 'We are giving the VC too freely, I think, but probably Mr Dalton has as good a claim as the others who have got the Cross for Rorke's Drift Defence.'

The colonial volunteers had been looked down on by the regular army as unmilitary and, more importantly to them, ungentlemanly. One of the colonial defenders was a hospital case, Swiss-born Christian Ferdinand Schiess. He had shown plenty of fighting spirit at the barricades and his case was pursued by the colonial government, keen that his contribution should be recognised. Finally, the VC was granted and Schiess received his Cross from Sir Garnet Wolseley on 3 February 1880 at Pietermaritzburg. The Battle of Rorke's Drift gained greater public significance than the disaster at Isandlwana, which was reflected in the eleven Victoria Crosses and five Distinguished Conduct Medals awarded.

Another contender for the Victoria Cross was Lieutenant Alan Coulson Gardner of the 14th Hussars. He was attached as staff officer in the Centre Column, which camped at Isandlwana. On 22 January, he was in the column that left the camp to go searching for the Zulu army in the hills 12 miles from the camp. After inconclusive skirmishing with what turned out to be decoys, Chelmsford sent Gardner back to camp with an order for the remainder of the force to join him.

Gardner arrived just as the Zulus began their attack on the camp. As the companies of the two 24th Battalions began to be overwhelmed, Gardner joined the exodus as they attempted to escape along Fugitives' Trail and across the Buffalo River. Here he met Captain Essex and Lieutenant Cochrane. Gardner scribbled a hasty note for the men at Rorke's Drift warning of the approach of the Zulu army and rode on to the Helpmekaar.

Leaving Essex and Cochrane at Helpmekaar, he rode on to Dundee to warn Colonel Evelyn Wood of the disaster. He had ridden 40 miles that day and had to change his horse. Although praised by senior officers, the prospect of a Victoria Cross proved unfounded. In fact, his fellow officers were disparaging and composed a little ditty: 'I very much fear, that the Zulus are near, so hang it, I'm off to Dundee.'

It is hard to tell whether Gardner was acting in his own interest but his ride was particularly tough. Later he was transferred to Colonel Wood's staff at Kambula in the north of Zululand. Wood did not like him and Gardner joined Redvers Buller as his number two in charge of the volunteer horsemen. He was put in charge of the Frontier Light Horse in their cattle rustling on 28 March at Hlobane. In a raid that became progressively dangerous as more Zulus joined the fray, Gardner was with Buller as they formed the rearguard to allow the volunteers escape down the Devil's Pass. His Horse was killed beneath him and he was mentioned in despatches by Buller. He made it back to Kambula and took part in the fighting next day, when he was wounded.

Redvers Buller also recommended another unlikely member of the rearguard: Veterinary Surgeon First Class Francis Duck. He had served in the Abyssinian campaign and the Frontier War of 1878, and, like Gardner, he was serving with the Frontier Light Horse and was with them as they ascended Hlobane Mountain. As the numbers of Zulus increased, the Volunteer Cavalry fell back to the only way off the plateau – Devil's Pass. Duck grabbed a rifle from a dead trooper and joined Buller in the rearguard to give the horsemen a chance to descend Devil's Pass. He came to Buller's notice and was later recommended for the Victoria Cross. His name was struck off by the Commander-in-Chief on the grounds 'that he had no right to be there'. Major General Frederick Smith paid Francis Duck a compliment when he quoted an example of his chivalrous fairness:

> When the Zulus were broken at Ulundi, the mounted troops were released from the square and went in pursuit. Duck stopped a Zulu with a bullet in the hip. He could easily have killed him with his revolver, but did not regard it as fair to a wounded man, so he fought the Zulu on foot with his own national weapon, the *assegai*.

Francis Duck was mentioned in despatches in the *London Gazette* on 5 July 1879. He served in the First Boer War and the Bechuanaland Expedition. When he retired in 1902, he became the first veterinary officer to receive a knighthood.

The first colonial to be gazetted for the VC was a New Zealand-born Irishman named Cecil Dudgeon D'Arcy. He was the son of a major serving in the 65th (Yorkshire) stationed in New Zealand. At an early age, Cecil D'Arcy came to South Africa and with the outbreak of the Ninth Frontier War, he volunteered for the Frontier Light Horse. By the time the Zulu War started, he had been commissioned and joined Evelyn Wood's column on the rugged northern border. He took part in the raid on Hlobane and was amongst those who were forced to retreat to Devil's Pass.

It was thanks to a rearguard, which included Cecil D'Arcy, that many managed to escape down the precipitous slope. Finally, the rearguard had to make a break themselves. On the way down, a huge rock fell on D'Arcy's horse, killing it. Forced to flee on foot, he had to contend with the Zulus who were hounding the retreating men. As he approached the bottom, he found a loose horse and had just mounted it when he saw a wounded trooper. Jumping off, he put the stricken man in the saddle and again took to his heels. As the Zulus closed in, Buller appeared on a horse, pulled D'Arcy up behind him and carried him to safety.

Buller's defeated horsemen travelled the 20 miles to the main camp at Kambula. Although the official casualty list puts the number of dead at ninety-one, subsequent research puts the number at nearer 130. In addition, some 200 to 300 native auxiliaries were slain. After Isandlwana, it was the most costly engagement of the Zulu War.

Buller was lavish in his recommendations for awards and included D'Arcy for his steadiness in the rearguard. Despite the fact that it was almost entirely a colonial force, the two VCs awarded for the Devil's Pass fight went to Redvers Buller and Major William Leet of the 13th (Somerset), both Imperial officers. When this was learned, there was a considerable outcry from the Natal Government and press that no volunteer had been so honoured.

It may have been with this in mind that Cecil D'Arcy received his Cross for a later action in which he failed in his attempt to save the life of a fallen trooper. D'Arcy attempted to lift a wounded trooper onto his horse and carry him to safety. Unfortunately, the horse threw them both and D'Arcy put out his back. Unable to lift the unconscious man, D'Arcy just managed to haul himself onto his mount and make his escape. As if to make up for the failure to honour the first colonial officer for his gallantry at Hlobane, the VC was bestowed on D'Arcy for his abortive attempt to save a stricken comrade. The ever-critical Sir Garnett Wolseley noted in his diary: 'I gave away the VC to Captain D'Arcy today on parade. I don't think he was a good case for the citation, as he did not succeed in saving the life of the man he dismounted to assist.'

The satisfaction of being awarded the VC was short-lived for D'Arcy. The years of living and campaigning in South Africa had taken their toll. D'Arcy suffered from malaria, bilharzias and asthma. By 1881, he had resigned his commission in somewhat controversial circumstances, due probably to his deteriorating state of health and bouts of drunkenness. D'Arcy accepted an invitation to stay with friends who lived in the mountains and who suggested the clear air would improve his condition. Ill, depressed and drinking too much, Cecil retired to his room after dinner on 3 August 1881. He was never seen alive again.

Extensive searches yielded nothing until, on 28 December, a native found a skeleton in a gully bearing a signet ring, scraps of clothing and a pocket watch, which identified the remains as those of the missing hero. An intriguing possibility has since come to light. A note was discovered in the Killie Campbell Africana Library suggesting that D'Arcy changed clothes with a dead man that he found lying in the snow. He was recognised from a photograph fifty-six years later by a cricketer in Newcastle, Natal. When confronted, D'Arcy is said to have begged the man not to make his identity known, wishing 'to remain dead to the world'.

The day before the battle of Ulundi, an officer performed an action that was not deemed worthy of a VC. Yet three other men did receive VCs for doing the same thing. On 28 May, Lieutenant Frederick Hutchinson of the 4th (King's Own) replaced Captain McCarthy of the Mounted Infantry who was invalided at the Battle of Kambula. On 3 July, the large force reached the banks of the White Umfolozi River. Chelmsford ordered Buller to take his horsemen across and scout the route to the nearby Zulu capital of Ulundi. Once they had forded the river, Buller's men spotted scattered parties of Zulus who, firing off a few rounds, turned and ran, presenting an irresistible target for the cavalrymen.

Buller suspected that the fleeing Zulus were leading his men into a trap and called a halt short of the long grass. Exhilarated by the chase, some horsemen did not hear the command and were suddenly confronted by some 3,000 warriors, who emerged from the cover of the grass. The group turned and retreated. Two had been killed but one red-clad mounted infantryman was lying on the ground, having been thrown from his horse. Despite the rapidly advancing Zulus, Captain William Beresford galloped back to the dazed and helpless man, dismounted and tried to put him onto his horse. The man, Sergeant Fitzmaurice of the 24th, was unable to help himself. Beresford managed to manhandle Fitzmaurice onto his horse, hurriedly mounted behind him and spurred the horse on. During this time, the Zulus had rapidly closed on the pair.

Through a combination of concussion and loss of blood, Fitzmaurice was unable to keep his balance and was in danger of falling off and pulling Beresford with him. Just as he was beginning to fear that he could not hold his burden much longer, help arrived in the shape of Sergeant Edmund O'Toole of the Frontier Light Horse. Having seen their danger, O'Toole had galloped forward to give covering fire. Keeping the Zulus at a distance, O'Toole was able to help Beresford complete his act of rescue. Finally, all three Irishman reached safety and

Lieutenant Colonel James Mauleverer, 30th (Cambridge) Regiment, led a charge at Inkerman but was rejected for the VC due to his rank.

Thomas Morley, 17th Lancers, took part in Charge of the Light Brigade and became a thorn in the side of the War Office for fifty years.

The *Sarah Sands*: a fire in mid-ocean was fought by men of the 54th Regiment. None were rewarded.

Lieutenant Colonel James Hagart, 7th Hussars, attempted to save Cornet
Willie Bankes. His recommendation for the VC was rejected.

Captain Charles Keyes, Umbeyla campaign. Although he was nominated for the VC, he recommended his two lieutenants instead.

Sergeant John Woods (third from left), 5th Northumberland Fusiliers, entered an Afghan fort and killed the occupants.

Private Frank Hayes and his mysterious DCM.

Captain John Beech was denied a VC thanks to Civil Service semantics.

Civilian James Watts rode for twelve hours through enemy territory to deliver message.

Clem Roberts saved Winston Churchill's life and was disappointed that he did not receive the VC.

George West – snobbery denied an exceptional naval career. He received a posthumous DCM.

Amyas Borton, RAF. Badly wounded, he managed to
bring his aircraft and observer back safely, but wasn't
awarded a VC.

John Simpson, Gallipoli. He used a donkey he found to carry wounded and became a symbol of bravery. He was killed but only received a mentioned in despatches.

Willie Doyle, the Irish priest who went out into no man's land to rescue the wounded.

Lieutenant Commander Robert Hichens. He received a DSO and bar, DSC and two bars but was turned down for a VC because he felt he had endangered his crew.

Lieutenant Colonel Blair 'Paddy' Mayne, SAS. A quiet man until aroused by alcohol. He was denied the VC but received a third bar to his DSO.

Group Captain Charles Pickard, RAF. He had a varied and exciting flying career, including overseeing the Amiens Prison Raid.

RSM Peter Ratcliffe, SAS – an inspirational leader but he was denied the VC.

Sergeant Dipprasad Pun, Gurkha Rifles.
He singlehandedly held thirty Taliban at bay.

returned to camp. Within hours, the camp learned that Lord Beresford had been recommended for the Victoria Cross and later, Trooper O'Toole. One who was not mentioned was Lieutenant Hutchinson, who had also ridden out to help Beresford. Just the previous day, Hutchinson had saved the life of Private Garstin, whose horse had been shot. Wheeling around, he had heaved Garstin up behind him and galloped off. For both acts, Hutchinson was recommended for the Victoria Cross by Colonel Evelyn Wood and Colonel Redvers Buller.

In January 1880, Lieutenant Colonel Frederick James Taggert Hutchinson wrote to Buller claiming the VC for his son. Buller replied, with the support of Lieutenant Edward Browne VC, that Hutchinson had behaved bravely but that 'a line had to be drawn somewhere'. In fact, Buller was not sure that any officers had been present when Fitzmaurice was rescued. In some exasperation, Buller passed the correspondence to the Military Secretary at Horse Guards and there the matter ended. Hutchinson left the Army on 1 May 1895 as a major. Ten days later, he was killed in a shooting accident.

Another would-be Victoria Cross recipient was Trooper William Barker of the Natal Carbineers. He and his comrades were in the camp at Isandlwana when 20,000 Zulus attacked. Barker ran to his immediate front to join his comrades as they faced the advancing Zulus. After firing about a dozen rounds, Barker heard a rushing sound behind and on looking round saw that the Zulus had penetrated the camp from the rear. Pressed from the front, the soldiers were forced back amongst the tents, where the Zulus were slaughtering the disorganised soldiers and natives.

Barker found his still-saddled horse and joined a couple of comrades in riding to where they thought there would be a rallying point on the Nek. Here they were met by an overwhelming force of Zulus. Turning back into the camp, Barker and a companion followed the direction in which they had seen an artillery carriage go. This was the only point that the Zulus had not yet closed and led to what later became known at the Fugitive's Trail. Chased for 6 miles over extremely rugged terrain, the mounted survivors reached the Buffalo River. This fast-moving river was in full spate and many who had survived the dangers of the trail perished beneath the swirling waters. Barker managed to cross safely and began to climb the steep slopes on the Natal bank. Here he joined Lieutenant Charlie Raw's Mounted Basutos, who were giving covering fire. The group then moved out of range of the Zulus on the far bank. The danger had not passed, for discontented relatives of the Zulus, who lived in the vicinity, attacked the survivors as they reached the Natal bank.

Looking back, Barker saw a distant figure scrambling on foot towards them. Thinking it was a friend, Barker left his companions and rode back down the hill. The struggling figure was not his friend but Lieutenant W.C.R. Higginson, the Adjutant of 2/3rd Natal Native Contingent. He had just left Lieutenants Melvill and Coghill on the shore with a promise that he would return with horses. With the hostile natives closing, Barker insisted the officer took his exhausted horse, as it was incapable of carrying them both up the steep slope. He obtained Higginson's promise that he would wait for him at the top of the hill. Higginson dug in his spurs and rode off to safety, while Barker struggled up the slope pursued by the same natives who had just killed Melvill and Coghill.

Meanwhile, Higginson had reached Charlie Raw and his group, who recognised Barker's horse. Certain that Barker was now dead, Higginson told them that he had found the horse down by the river. The horse was relinquished in exchange for a spare Basuto pony and Higginson rode off to the safety of Helpmekaar, where he made his report.

Raw and his companions rode back towards the river to check for any survivors and came upon Trooper Barker still running for his life. He had been pursued for about 3 miles, managing to fire the occasional round to keep natives at a distance.

Within a few days, the truth of Higginson's escape and his supposedly humane gesture in searching for horses for Lieutenants Melvill and Coghill became well known. To avoid the shame and ignominy of his action, Higginson left Helpmekaar, complete with a black eye, and quietly disappeared into obscurity. And there it would have ended but for a visit paid on 17 December 1881 to the Natal Carbineers by the outgoing military commander, Sir Evelyn Wood. During his speech to the officers he mentioned:

> I have only now heard of a gallant act performed by a straggler, whose late arrival is well explained by his having, during the retreat, given up his horse to an officer, who was exhausted. Into this matter, it will be my pleasure to enquire more.

Trooper, now Sergeant, William Barker was recommended by Wood for the Victoria Cross. There had already been a reaction in Whitehall over the seemingly lavish dispensing of the Cross and it could not have been such a surprise for Wood to receive the following reply:

> I am directed by the Field Marshal Commanding in Chief to acknowledge your letter of the 6th instant, and to acquaint you in

reply, that statements re: Trooper Barker, Natal Carbineers, at the battle of Isandlwana, on 22 January 1879, having carefully been considered, His Royal Highness desires me to state that, while Trooper Barker's conduct on the occasion referred to is deserving of every commendation, there does not appear to be sufficient ground, according to the terms of the statute, for recommending him for the distinction of the Victoria Cross.

Another well-merited Victoria Cross could very easily have been overlooked and forgotten were it not for the intervention of General Sir Garnet Wolseley. Never a supporter of the highest award for gallantry since he was overlooked for one by Sir Colin Campbell, his Indian Mutiny commander. In this instance, he pulled out all the stops to have a grave injustice reversed.

Sergeant Anthony Booth, a Nottingham man, joined the 80th Staffordshire Volunteers in 1864. When the invasion of Zululand began on 12 January 1879, the 80th were stationed at Derby in northern Natal with orders to protect the settlements around Luneburg. In March, Luneburg was occupied by five companies of the 80th Regiment. Supplies for this garrison were sent from Derby, the road from which crossed the Intombi River. On 7 March, a company of the regiment under the command of Captain David Harry Moriarty left Luneburg to meet the Derby convoy and bring it in. On reaching the drift, or ford, on the Intombi, it was found impossible for the convoy to cross as heavy rains had swollen the river. For two days, the escort and wagoners laboured and managed to get two of the wagons across the river to the south bank, but the continuous heavy rain meant that there was no alternative other than to wait for the river to subside.

On 11 March, Major Tucker, accompanied by Lieutenant Henry Harward, rode to the drift to assess the situation. He saw that there were still sixteen wagons on the north bank and expressed his concern that they were not laagered correctly. They were formed into an inverted 'V' from the river and the gap between the wagons was too far apart. Moriarty acknowledged this but the adverse conditions dictated the formation and nothing was done to improve the defence of the encampment. Tucker returned to Luneburg, leaving Harward to assist Moriarty.

Moriarty's men, who were tired and wet, stripped off their wet clothes and fell into a deep sleep under shelter for the first time in days. At about 4.00 am, Harward was awakened by the sound of a distant shot. He ordered Booth to alert the other bank as no one had stirred, not even the sentries. After some yelling, Booth managed to arouse someone, who spread the warning, but the camp continued to sleep.

At about 4.45 am, another shot rang out close by. Booth jumped from the wagon to see the Zulus emerge from the mist and fire a volley into Moriarty's tent before rushing in with a chilling cry of '*Usutho!*' In seconds they overwhelmed the sleeping camp. As naked and partially clothed soldiers struggled from their tents, they were clubbed and stabbed to death in the hellish melee of frightened cattle and terrified men. Some men plunged into the river but few reached the safety of the far bank. Those who did took shelter behind the flimsy barrier of the two wagons.

Booth and his comrades scrambled beneath the wagons and started firing at the mass of Zulus. In jostling to take cover, Booth had his helmet knocked off, which rolled towards the river. He put his arm on the rear wheel to steady his aim and fired as fast as he could. He noticed that he was next to Lieutenant Harward's pony, which was tied to the wagon. Harward emerged from his tent and saw that the Zulus, attracted by the fire from Booth and his men, were crossing the river further upstream. Perhaps gripped by a vision of another Isandlwana, Harward blurted out, 'Fire away, lads. I'll be ready in a minute.' He then pulled himself onto his unsaddled pony and rode off up the road to Luneburg, followed by most of his men and a few escapees. Booth was shocked by this behaviour: 'leaving his command at the moment of extreme peril, an act positively incredible in a British officer'.

Booth later wrote that only eight of his company remained. They were joined by some of the men who crossed the river, who donned whatever clothing was available and armed themselves. Seeing his position was hopeless, Sergeant Booth, assisted by Lance Corporal Burgess, formed the remaining men into a square and began to retire towards Luneburg. Booth was later complimented for choosing this formation instead of an extended line. Each time the Zulus threatened the small band, they were kept at a distance by the group's volley fire. Apart from four men who decided to break away and take a short cut only to run into the Zulus, Booth managed to bring his men to safety.

While Sergeant Booth was calmly extricating his men from almost certain death, his superior officer, Lieutenant Harward, had galloped to Luneburg, arriving at 6.30 am. He roused Major Tucker with the words, 'The camp is in the hands of the enemy; they are all slaughtered and I have galloped in for my life.' According to Tucker, Harward then fell on the bed in a dead faint. After being revived, Harward told the story of the attack on the camp. Tucker ordered 150 men to march to the drift. Inexplicably, he made no mention of Sergeant Booth's commendable exploit even though he came upon the party at a farmhouse. Booth volunteered to accompany Tucker's command, but was told that he had done enough.

In the aftermath of the disaster, there was a considerable amount of covering up of what was an embarrassing episode for the regiment. In his report, Major Tucker made no mention that he felt that the camp had been inadequately laagered. Furthermore, he praised Harward's efforts in giving covering fire to enable some men to escape across the river. These two reports were the basis of Lord Chelmsford's report to the War Office, which was not received in London until 21 April. As reports from NCOs were not required, the truth would appear to have been contained within the regiment.

With the Zulus defeated, the 80th were involved in much of the mopping-up operations under the new commander-in-chief, General Sir Garnet Wolseley. In November, they took part in the attack on Sekhukhune's stronghold and were the first troops to reach the summit, gaining high praise from Wolseley. Indeed, the 80th had been closely associated with the commander since his arrival, as they supplied his personal escort.

By the middle of December, the regiment was concentrated at Pretoria and it was here that months of resentment and shame came to the boil. Three survivors of the Intombi River massacre wrote to Wolseley on 20 December 1879 to set the record straight and 'to be of good service to Colour Sergeant Booth'. This was followed by a belated recommendation from the newly promoted Lieutenant Colonel Tucker for the Distinguished Conduct Medal to be awarded to Booth. As this was the result of Wolseley's enquiry in response to the three survivors' testimony, Tucker was asked why he had not previously recommended his sergeant for a medal. Tucker was then forced to explain that to do so would have brought to light the 'far different conduct of Lieutenant Harward'.

On 26 December, the whole regiment was paraded prior to leaving for England. Sir Garnet Wolseley took the salute and, in a most unusual ceremony, presented Colour Sergeant Booth with a revolver, holster, belt and knife, which were donated by European settlers. On the same day, Wolseley forwarded his personal recommendation that Booth should be awarded the Victoria Cross.

On 14 February 1880, as a result of Wolseley's investigations, Lieutenant Harward was arrested and taken to Pietermaritzburg, where he was charged with misbehaviour before the enemy. Much to Wolseley's disgust, the court martial accepted Harward's version of events and he was acquitted and allowed to return to his regiment.

Wolseley could not alter the verdict of the court but he did add his own trenchant view. When the findings and Wolseley's comments reached London, the Duke of Cambridge instructed them to be read out as a general order to every regiment. With his army career in tatters, Harward had little option but to resign his commission.

Colour Sergeant Anthony Booth was summoned from his station in Ireland to Windsor Castle, where Queen Victoria presented him with the Victoria Cross on 26 June 1880. His citation reads:

> For his gallant conduct on 12th March 1879, during the Zulu attack on the Intombi River, in having when considerably outnumbered by the enemy, rallied a few men on the south bank of the river, and covered the retreat of fifty soldiers and others for a distance of three miles. The officer commanding the 80th Regiment reports that, had it not been for the coolness displayed by this non-commissioned officer, not one man would have escaped.

It is hard to find a campaign with so many anomalies and hidden acts of gallantry as the Zulu War. Booth is a good case. Another is Private Samuel Wassall, also of the 80th (Staffordshire), the only VC from the Battle of Isandlwana, if Melvill and Coghill's posthumous VCs of 1907 can't be counted. He had volunteered for the Mounted Infantry five months before the Isandlwana disaster and was one of the lucky ones who was mounted as he left the camp and escaped down Fugitive's Trail to the Buffalo River. His act of bravery was observed by Captain William Barton of the Natal Native Horse who was able to compose a statement twenty days later, which read, in part:

> As I approached the river, a man in the Mounted Infantry was riding in front of me, and I also saw at the same time another man of the Mounted Infantry struggling in the river and he called out his comrade's name; he was apparently drowning. The Zulus were at that time firing at our people from above us, others were down on the bank of the river stabbing others of our people on both sides of where I was. The man of the Mounted Infantry, who rode down in front of me, dismounted, left his horse on the Zulu side and sprang into the river to save his comrade.
>
> I consider this man to have performed a most gallant and courageous act, in trying to save his comrade at the almost certain risk of his own life. I crossed the river myself, about the same time and did not think it possible that either of these two men could have escaped alive; indeed I spoke some days afterwards to Lieutenant Walsh of the Mounted Infantry of the circumstances which I had witnessed and I spoke of it to him as evidence of my having seen two of his men lost at the Buffalo River.

So, initially, Barton told Walsh of the incident in the belief that he was merely reporting the certain deaths of two of Walsh's men. However, a few days later, when Barton was visiting the makeshift hospital at Helpmekaar, a Private Westwood, ill in bed, overheard Barton recount the gallant conduct of the unknown soldier. Westwood immediately cried out, identifying himself as the one who had been rescued and Wassall as his saviour.

It was then that Barton decided to report the matter in writing. The written statements of Barton, Westwood and Walsh were then submitted to Captain Edward Browne, 24th, the officer commanding the Mounted Infantry. Browne wasted no time. On the day he received the statements, he immediately wrote to the officer commanding Mounted Troops, No. 3 Column, Lieutenant Colonel John Cecil Russell, a special duty officer of the 12th Lancers:

> Sir, I have the honour to forward the accompanying reports for submission to HE The Lieutenant General Commanding (Chelmsford). … As the identity of the man mentioned, viz. Pte Wassall 80th Regiment, 1st Squadron Mounted Infantry, has now in my opinion been fully established, I now respectively submit for the consideration of HE The Lieutenant General Commanding, the circumstances of the case and hope that he may deem the gallant action performed by Pte Wassall worthy of being rewarded with the decoration of the Victoria Cross.

Russell, following correct procedure, in turn wrote to Colonel Richard Glyn, the commander of No. 3 Column, who was still entrenched in appalling conditions at Rorke's Drift with what was left of his shattered command:

> Sir, I have the honour to forward to you a letter and correspondence I have received from Captain Browne, commanding 1st Squadron Mounted Infantry, with reference to the gallant conduct of the man mentioned in the margin. This man appears to have behaved in an exceptionally brave manner, in saving the life of his comrade, and I trust that it may be considered right to bring his name forward for a special mark of distinction.

With the loss of so many officers and men of his regiment at Isandlwana, Colonel Glyn was a depressed man with much on his mind. On 18 February, and without comment, he merely sent the statements off to the military secretary of the Lieutenant General Commanding, Lord Chelmsford. The bundle would have travelled by despatch rider, carrying other correspondence, over rough terrain and several swollen rivers, the 130 miles to Pietermaritzburg, where Chelmsford had his headquarters. Although it was 260 miles for the return journey, and bearing in mind that Chelmsford must, if anything, have been even more preoccupied with the Isandlwana disaster than Glyn, within eight days back came a waspish reply from Chelmsford. It reflected the animosity existing between him and Glyn for Chelmsford was seeking scapegoats for Isandlwana, and Glyn was in the frame. Without bothering to use a separate sheet of notepaper, and in his own hand, Chelmsford had scrawled an abrupt rebuke across the bottom of Russell's letter: 'In cases like the one under reference, it is absolutely necessary that you should yourself enquire into the matter and express an opinion as to the accuracy of the statements made. Please return without delay.'

The beleagued Glyn could be equally scratchy as his general and circumstances had also changed. The Mounted Squadron were no longer attached to Glyn's command and had been transferred north to No. 4 Column, commanded by Colonel Evelyn Wood VC. Without further ado, Glyn passed on the bundle to Wood, scrawling under Chelmsford's comments: 'Officer Commanding No. 4 Column. Passed on to you as the Mounted Infantry is under your command.'

On receipt of the papers, Wood read between the lines and decided to pass part of the ball back to Glyn, to whom he wrote on 9 March:

> It would appear that Pte Westwood is still serving under your command – perhaps you will enquire to his statement, and forward your remarks direct to the Military Secretary. I have ordered the attendance of Lieutenant Walsh and Pte Wassall at this camp, and will forward the result of my enquiries to the Military Secretary.

In turn, taking his time and still cantankerous, Glyn replied to Wood on 28 March: 'Full enquiries have been made about Pte Westwood but he cannot be traced in connection with any corps in this command.'

Westwood, it seems, had disappeared and the ball was back in Wood's court. The possible award of the Victoria Cross to a brave and deserving man was in danger of being lost due to indifference and pettiness. Wood then instructed his staff officer, Captain Maude, to return the bundle back to Colonel Russell, with a note: 'For further enquiry and report.'

The next day, Russell, now seemingly as disinterested as Glyn, replied to the effect that although Westwood had been sick in Helpmekaar, it was now believed that he had been taken to Pietermaritzburg. Wood again wasted no time and wrote a letter, dated 5 April, to the Officer Commanding Troops, Pietermaritzburg requesting him to track down Westwood. It was now almost two months since Barton had written his first statement and, presumably, Wassall was aware of the stir he was causing in high circles. At length, Westwood was found in hospital and brought before the Pietermaritzburg District Magistrate to make another statement.

This time, Westwood's account was recorded verbatim and not transposed into a formal style, as had obviously been the case in his initial evidence taken down by Walsh. From then on, events moved quickly and on 17 June, Samuel Wassall's citation appeared in the *London Gazette*. It was not until after the Zulu War was officially over, on 1 September, that Wassall finally received his VC. General Garnet Wolseley, who succeeded Chelmsford, travelled from the defeated Zulu capital, Ulundi, to Pretoria in the Transvaal. On the way, he stopped at Utrecht to perform one more duty. The 80th Regiment assembled and watched as Samuel Wassall received his well-merited VC.

The odyssey of Wassall's recommendation had been tenuous and but for the perseverance of men like Barton, Browne and Wood, a brave man would have gone unknown and unrewarded.

Chapter 9

The Last Two Decades

The Anglo-Zulu War lasted six months and netted twenty-four Victoria Crosses, with several worthy rejections. In stark contrast, the Second Afghan War lasted just under three years and produced only sixteen Crosses. The Duke of Cambridge had been dismayed at the number of Zulu War VCs that had been awarded and commented that 'we are giving the VC very freely I think'. The Queen's approval of a new warrant in April 1881 included the phrase 'marked gallantry in the performance of an act of duty'. This coincided with a complete change at the head of the civil side of the War Office and saw a tightening up of the awarding of the Victoria Cross. It also saw some applicants who previously would have been eligible for the award but were either brevetted, mentioned in despatches or received the Distinguished Conduct Medal. During the 1880s, in eight campaigns, only twenty-three VCs were awarded as opposed to forty-eight during the 1870s.

On 29 March 1880, Lieutenant General Donald Stewart began his march from Kandahar to Ghazni with 7,200 troops and 6,400 camp followers. As with such a mixed column, it developed into an extended line of about 6 miles. On 19 April, the head of the column reached Ahmed Khel, 23 miles south of Ghazni. On the left they were overlooked by a series of hills filled with an Afghan force of 1,000 horsemen and 12,000 armed tribesmen on foot. The attack came swiftly and caught Stewart's men unawares. Before the regiments could complete their deployment, a huge mass of tribesmen appeared over the crest of the hills and immediately charged straight down on the unprepared infantry.

The 59th (East Lancashire) Regiment was mid-deployment before they had time to fix bayonets when it was hit by a wave of Afghan swordsmen. They had been ordered to wheel inwards to enable the artillery to open fire. A young subaltern named Humphrey Martin Twynam of the 59th saw that the sergeant major of the 60th Rifles had been badly wounded in the knee and was left behind. Twynam ran to the NCO as the Ghazi closed in but he was unable to lift the 16-stone sergeant major, who shouted, 'For God's sake, Sir, go back to your regiment; you can do me no good and I am too heavy to carry.'

With the Ghazis close by, Twynam opened fire, killing three. With three or four more almost upon him, the artillery opened fire with grapeshot, killing the sergeant major and accounting for the rest of the Ghazi. Miraculously, Twynam escaped unharmed, although another discharge of grape narrowly missed him. With the Ghazis determined to hack him to pieces, Twynam had time to turn and fire at five or six assailants.

By the end of this violent hour-long fight, the Afghans had lost about 3,000 against a British loss of 117 killed or wounded. That night, the regiment sat Twynam on the wall of a well and marched past him in a torchlit parade, joined by many from the 60th Rifles. His fellow officers were unanimous in recommending him for the Victoria Cross.

Stewart waited long enough to bury the dead before resuming the march to Ghazni. A halt was called for three days and then the march resumed towards Kabul. The tribesmen, smarting from the defeat at Ahmed Khel, gathered some 6,000 at the villages of Urzoo and Shilgut ready to seek revenge. Once again, Sub Lieutenant Twynam was involved and gave a good account of himself in seeing off the Afghans.

The application for Twynam's Victoria Cross came to naught as the colonel of the regiment refused to make an application. General Stewart was unable to take the matter further but did mention Twynam in his report to General Roberts.

During the Anglo Boer War, Twynam received the DSO and served in Baden-Powell's South African Constabulary. For his service in the Transvaal, he received a mention in despatches from Baden-Powell for 'zealous work and energy in command of 'A' Division'.

On 19 May 1880, during the Afghan War, an act that merited the Victoria Cross was carried out by Captain Henry Kilgour and Colour Sergeant John Woods of the 5th (Northumberland) Fusiliers. Under the command of Brigadier General Doran, about 700 troops crossed the Kabul River near Jalalabad to oppose the Safi tribesmen. Marching out a short distance, they found about 2,000 Safis holding some ruined buildings and enclosures. With the 5th Fusiliers on the left and the 12th (Suffolk) on the right, they advanced within 900 yards of the enemy's centre, with a small fort (tower) on the flank. The mountain artillery opened up and the Safis began to retreat to the village of Beniga. About twenty-two Afghans, seeing their retreat to the hills cut off, occupied the small fort. Once again, the mountain guns fired at the fort and three defenders ran out. Sergeant Woods wrote a statement describing the action:

> At the taking of the tower, on 19 May 1880, myself and Pte. Openshaw charged into a small place at the foot of the tower – Pte. Openshaw shot one and before he had time to recover himself another of the enemy attacked him and gave him a severe wound on the wrist. Col. Rowland got wounded at this time.
>
> I also noticed Pte. Longworth of the 12th Regiment on my right engaged with the enemy. I saw one of the enemy making a severe cut at him with one of those long knives, and saw he could not parry it. I tried to do so but failed as the knife gave him a severe wound on the shoulder. My sword (bayonet) had got bent a few seconds later before this by one of the enemy jumping out of the tower at me. I transfixed him with my sword and the weight of his body bent it in the manner described. I then helped to dispatch any of the enemy I saw at the bottom of the tower.
>
> I then made a charge for a hole in the tower and was met at the entrance by a fellow I took to be one of the priests as he flung a book of the Koran in my face and attacked me at the same time with a hatchet; he flung the hatchet at me but I warded the blow with my rifle. I must have put the sword through his heart, as his death was instantaneous. After withdrawing my sword, my foot slipped and I fell – about four of them caught my sword and tried to drag me in but my rifle was loaded so I pulled the trigger and blew their hands and fingers off. I at once got to my feet and engaged with the nearest fellow. I put my sword through his windpipe and the weight of his body falling before I could withdraw it bent it more and made it useless.
>
> I got the fellow's sword and shield and used that. They then commenced to hurl their rifles at me and one struck me on the forearm and gave a bruise which was rather painful.
>
> One fellow fired at me inside, he was kneeling down but fortunately missed me. I thought it had hit Capt. Kilgour who was just in rear of me, I forgot to mention his name before. He was second into the tower and it is not his fault that he was not first and did some splendid work when he did get in. When I first got into the tower, I thought there were about twenty of the enemy there, but I could not exactly say. I can't remember anyone but Capt. Kilgour following me into the tower as I was much too occupied with the work that had to be done.

Both men were recommended for the Victoria Cross but this was rejected by General Frederick Roberts, the Commander-in-Chief. Instead, Kilgour received a brevet of major and Woods was awarded the DCM, which he received from the Queen at Osborne House the following year.

Following the defeat of the Zulus in 1879, the British had to then contend with the Boers, who wished independence for the Transvaal. Having used the Transvaal during the Zulu War, the British were in no hurry to leave. This provoked another war for which the British had no stomach and ended in humiliation. One of the deeply shaming episodes was the defeat on 27 February 1881 of the British on Majuba Hill. The only men to come out with credit were the medical teams. One was Surgeon Edward Mahon of HMS *Boadicea*, who landed with the Navy Brigade. He was attached to Major General Sir George Pomeroy Colley's force of 405 men who occupied the crest of the steep-sided Majuba Hill. He later met with Henry Colley, Sir George's brother, explaining:

> I saw him near the centre of the plateau on top of the hill. The Boers asked me to identify him, and this I did. He was only wounded once, and that through the top of the skull. Death must have been instantaneous. From the direction of the wound, he must have been facing Boers when hit.

The following is an extract from *The Royal Navy, a History 1857–1900* by William Laird Clowes:

> Earlier in the day a hospital had been established behind a ridge near the centre of the plateau. The enemy crowned the rocks, and fired upon all indiscriminately, shooting down a doctor while he was caring for the wounded. Perceiving how things had gone, Surgeon Mahon, who but lately had quitted [Commander] Francis Romilly in order to cross to his Commander's side, and to save further slaughter of the wounded and non-wounded combatants, hoisted a white flag. All the fugitives, however, were not then clear of the top. And firing continued on the summit. To avoid the bullets, Mahon and Assistant Sick-Berth Attendant Bevis, who was with him, lay down till the plateau was clear of their flying friends and until the enemy was within a few paces from them. When they rose, they were not molested, and were suffered to carry poor Romilly to the hospital from the point where he had lain sheltered on the south-west front.
>
> Throughout that afternoon and the following night Mahon remained on the mountain, seeking out and attending to the wounded, and receiving much kindly help from the enemy.

He took it upon himself to send for blue-jacket prisoners to carry Romilly back to camp; but, soon after they had started – they were ordered back by the enemy. The result being that the unfortunate Commander had to lie in the open during the whole of the wet, dark and chilly night of the 27th. … Mahon, who reached camp at 5.00 pm on 28th, with five ambulances full of wounded, behaved throughout with magnificent devotion and gallantry, and was specially promoted. In the opinion of all those who were left on the fatal hill, he deserved the Victoria Cross.

Both Mahon and Bevis were recommended for the Victoria Cross, but the GOC Natal, Major General Sir Evelyn Wood, rejected the recommendation with a letter to Horse Guards, in which he stated:

I have carefully perused the whole of the enclosed correspondence relative to the conduct of Surgeon Mahon and Sick Berth Attendant Bevis and the opinion I have formed there from is that the circumstances do not justify me in recommending either surgeon or Bevis for the distinction of the Victoria Cross; if Surgeon Mahon and Bevis had been soldiers I would have suggested that the surgeon should be commended for his praiseworthy conduct and that the man should receive the Distinguished Service Medal.

Bevis received the Conspicuous Gallantry Medal while Mahon was promoted to staff surgeon.

Another VC hopeful was Lieutenant Ian Hamilton of the 92nd Highlanders. He spoke three languages, including Hindi, was charming and kind. He was also twice recommended for the Victoria Cross. As a lieutenant he fought on Majuba, was badly wounded on the wrist and taken prisoner. The injury left Hamilton with a permanently disabled hand. He was recommended for a Victoria Cross but it was denied as it was 'not quite VC-enough' and also, 'as a young man he would have many opportunities in the future to earn recognition'.

Twenty years later, he was again put forward for the Victoria Cross for his leadership of the 7th Brigade at Elandslaagte, one of the few early victories for the British Army. As a 47-year-old brigadier, he was regarded as being too senior and old to be considered. This was the excuse made by General Buller, who decided not to forward the recommendation to higher authority. As Buller disliked Hamilton, there was personal enmity in his decision to block Hamilton's application.

The only soldier to be awarded a gallantry medal for the Battle of El Teb was Private Frank Hayes of the 10th Hussars. He was born in Dublin in 1856 and joined the 10th Hussars at Canterbury as a bandsman in 1877. It is not clear what instrument he played; possibly a bugle. He served in India and later in the Afghan campaign. The 10th Hussars left India in February 1884 but were diverted to Suakin to take part in the Sudan war against Osman Digna's Dervishes. As they were without horses, their former commander, General Valentine Baker Pasha, handed over 300 mounts from his Egyptian Gendarmerie. Within a week, on 29 February, the 10th Hussars were engaged in the Battle of El Teb.

The infantry squares held firm and the Dervishes were driven back to their defences. The cavalry, instead of waiting for the Dervishes to break themselves on the squares, charged groups of the enemy who had not taken part in the charge. The result of this piecemeal action was they lost twenty killed and forty-eight wounded.

When the Dervishes finally retreated, the 10th went in pursuit. In rather strange circumstances, Private Frank Hayes challenged a Dervish chief who was attempting to escape. There are various published accounts of Hayes's gallantry, one of which is recounted in Cassell's *History of the War in the Soudan*:

> Private Hayes showed great courage in the second charge here, in dismounting, attacking, and killing a chief who was endeavouring to escape. Finding that his horse would not face the spear, he undauntedly attacked the Arab on foot, and killed him in single combat.

Other accounts record that Hayes, a noted pugilist, found himself surrounded and, being unable to wield his sword effectively on horseback, dismounted and dispersed his assailants with his fists. Whether his action was witnessed by his superior officers is not recorded, but it seems somewhat far-fetched that he should dismount to take on such fanatics as the Dervishes.

El-Teb was followed with another battle at Tamai on 13 March and within two days, *Punch* published a poem about Hayes entitled 'A Tale of the Tenth Hussars'; part of it reads:

> For the Tenth had another hero, all ripe for the General's praise,
> Who was called to the front that evening by the name of Trooper Hayes;
> He had slashed his way to fortune, when scattered, unhorsed, alone,
> And in saving the life of a comrade had managed to guard his own.
>
> The General spoke out bravely, as ever a soldier can–
> 'The Army's proud of your valour; the Regiment's proud of their man!'
> Then across that lonely desert, at the close of the General's praise,
> Came a cheer, then a quick short tremble on the lips of Trooper Hayes.

'Speak out,' said the kindly Colonel, 'if you've anything, lad, to say;
Your Queen and your dear old country shall hear what you've done
   to-day!'
But the Trooper gnawed his chin-strap, then sheepishly hung his head;
'Speak out, old chap!' said his comrades. With an effort, at last, he said–

'I came to the front with my pals here, the boys, and the brave old tars,
I've fought for my Queen and country, and rode with the Tenth Hussars;
I'm proud of the fine old regiment!' then the Colonel shook his hand–
'So I'll ask one single favour from my Queen and my native land!

'There sits by your side on the Staff, sir, a man we are proud to own!
He was struck down first in the battle, but was never heard to groan;
If I've done aught to deserve it,' – then the General smiled, 'Of Course!'
'Give back to the Tenth their Colonel – the Man on the old White Horse!

The 'Man on the old White Horse' was General Valentine Baker Pasha, who had been dismissed from the British Army in 1875 for allegedly indecently assaulting a young lady in a railway carriage. The full poem was widely reprinted throughout every paper in the country due to the very opportune references to him and did much to rehabilitate Valentine Baker in his final years. It is still not clear whether Frank Hayes actually performed his pugilistic feat or whether it was a ploy to reinstate Baker among his peers. If Hayes did dismount and singlehandedly fight and kill the Dervish chief, then he would be eligible for the Victoria Cross. The press was always sceptical about Baker's involvement with the young lady as he did not offer a defence. Despite his controversial status, Baker continued to serve British interests in an unofficial capacity in order to obtain his pardon. He eventually received his reinstatement but tragically the news reached him a few days after his death in 1887. On 13 March 1885, Frank Hayes was invested the DCM by the Queen at Windsor Castle. He left the 10th Hussars on 6 August 1887, after the horse he was riding rolled over on his leg, crushing it. When he had recovered, he immediately joined the Scots Guards as a bandsman on 19 August 1887, and stayed with them until 21 April 1899. He was medically discharged due to problems with his damaged leg.

After the defeat of the Egyptian Army at Tel-el-Kebir in 1882, British officers were seconded to reform and lead what had been a ramshackle force of *fellaheen* led by ineffective and disinterested Egyptian officers. From the years 1882 to 1899, the British managed to turn this poorly led rabble into an efficient fighting unit. Witness the re-conquest of the Sudan from 1896 to 1899 – one of the main British commitments to the Middle East at the height of Empire.

One such officer was Captain John Robert Beech. He had studied at the Edinburgh Veterinary College and joined the Army as a veterinary surgeon, the only means available to him. He worked in Egypt buying horses and camels for the Government, served through the Anglo-Egyptian War, the Gordon Relief Expedition and the Sudan War. He was the only man to receive a seven-clasp medal for the latter campaign: Toski 1889, Gemaizah 1888, Abu Klea, The Nile 1884–85, El Teb, Tamaai, Suakin 1884 and Tel-el-Kebir. On 30 May 1891, he applied for a commission with the 20th Hussars, which was granted.

On 6 April 1891, he was in command of the Egyptian cavalry, which led the force commanded by Colonel Holled-Smith. They occupied the ruins of Tokar, long abandoned by the Mahdists. There were no British troops involved save officers and NCOs, but there was Royal Naval support from HMS *Dolphin*. A sharp fight took place at a nearby village, during which one of the British officers was killed.

Meanwhile, the transport animals, deserted by their drivers, had stampeded, but most were driven back by the staff. The Dervishes' cavalry had spotted this and got among the animals. Beech saw this and led his horsemen into the confusion of man and beast. There was severe hand-to-hand fighting, during which Beech saw an Egyptian officer, Bimbashi (Major) Millazim Awal Ali eff Kamil, unhorsed and severely wounded. Three Dervishes moved in to finish him off. Beech spurred his horse and galloped forward, killed two with his sword but was badly wounded. The third tried to escape but was killed by another cavalryman.

For this gallant act, he was recommended by two senior officers – the Duke of Cambridge and Sir Redvers Buller – for the Victoria Cross. This gave the War Office another problem. Although Captain Beech was in the British Army, Britain was not fighting the Mahdists, and Whitehall was put in a quandary about how to reward one of their officers. The memos went back and forth but for some reason the Duke of Cambridge was not consulted. Finally he saw the papers and on 1 April 1891, Major General Harman, Military Secretary at the War Office, wrote to Sir Ralph Wood Thompson, the Permanent Under-Secretary:

> HRH [Duke of Cambridge] had now seen this recommendation that Captain J.R. Beech, CMG, 20th Hussars, should be awarded the VC for his conspicuous gallantry at the action of Tokar. HRH considers this one of the most deserving cases for this honourable distinction that has ever been brought to his notice and as this individual act on the part of a British officer he considers that the fact of his having been at the time lent for service to HH the Khedive and performing service with Egyptian Troops only, should

not be a bar to his receiving this coveted award, as the gallantry was personal and independent of the general operations that were directed under the orders of the Khedive.

The Secretary of State, Edward Stanhope, had the final say when he wrote on 1 May:

> After much consideration and some consultation with my colleagues I have reluctantly come to the conclusion that this cannot be granted. I am sorry to have to refuse it after the warm terms in which it is recommended by HRH but I cannot distinguish it from other decorations sufficiently to day that it ought to be given for a service performed with the Egyptian Army in an operation in which British troops were not engaged.

General Harman wrote to the Khedive on 4 June he turned down Beech's VC application but recommended the following solution:

> HRH is, however, much gratified to have been able to mark his high appreciation of Captain Beech's distinguished service by recommending him for the Distinguished Service Order, which HM has been graciously pleased to confer upon him.

Having suggested an Egyptian award, Whitehall then decided that granting the British DSO was perfectly in order!

This confusion was highlighted in 1898 when Captain the Hon. Alexander Hore-Ruthven, then on detached command of the Camel Corps, saved the life of an Egyptian officer at the Battle of Gedarif in the Sudan, in which no British troops were involved. With no hesitation, Hore-Ruthven's application was recognised as a VC action and his Cross was gazetted on 26 February 1899. Could it be that Beech, a humble vet, was overlooked while Hore-Ruthven would soon become the Earl of Gowrie?

Chapter 10

African Land Grab

The Anglo-Boer War 1899–1902 was a continuation of the First Anglo-Boer War of 1881. Pressure was put on the Boers when it was found that gold had been discovered in large quantities in the Transvaal. This led to the humiliation of the Jameson Raid, which inflamed the Boers and prepared them for war with their ambitious neighbours. As the incoming Secretary of State for Colonies, Joseph Chamberlain remarked, 'South African policy in the past had been one long blunder from the imperial standpoint.'

It was about to get worse, with a protracted war against the Boer republics that did little to enhance Britain's standing in the world. The three-year-long war produced seventy-eight Victoria Crosses, the highest number since the Indian Mutiny. Over 2,000 Distinguished Conduct Medals were awarded to some men who previously would have received the Cross. One man, who laid claim to not just one Victoria Cross but two, was the Canadian politician Samuel Hughes.

Born in 1853 in Canada West, now Ontario, he was the son of an Orangeman from County Tyrone and an Ulster-Scottish mother. He grew up with all the prejudices of his parents, combining hard work with aggression. Hughes sat on the executive board of the local branch of the Loyal Orange Order and throughout his career was able to use the Orangemen to provide a reliable group of voters when seeking election to the House of Commons. Whenever he visited Toronto, he could not resist brawling with the Irish Catholic immigrants. He was a teacher for ten years and then became owner of a newspaper that supported the militia in putting down the North-West Rebellion led by the Frenchman Louis Riel. This far-west area became another Canadian province, Saskatchewan.

Hughes entered Parliament in 1892 and when Prime Minister Laurier gave half-hearted support for sending Canadian troops to fight in South Africa, he appointed Sam Hughes as one of the commanders. Hughes, in exasperation at the delay, offered to fund a 1,000-strong volunteer contingent to send to South Africa. Laurier backed down and a government-sponsored Canadian force was sent to the Cape Colony. Ironically, the ultra-imperialist Hughes was in constant conflict with the British Army and he developed contempt for the British military. He felt that Canadians, who were brought up on the frontier, were tougher and better soldiers than the British – something that did not endear him to the British authorities.

In May 1900, Hughes was appointed Intelligence Officer and Assistant Adjutant General to Warren's Scouts, who were tasked with crossing the Orange River and attacking Piet de Villiers's force. Instead, on 27 May, de Villiers attacked the Canadian camp. Hughes, aroused by the gunfire, led a counter-attack that drove the Boers back with an expensive cost of twenty-three dead and thirty-three wounded.

Hughes was an energetic commander who led his men on extensive scouts, but with little result. He campaigned constantly to be awarded the Victoria Cross for actions in which he had supposedly taken part. By recommending himself for the gallantry award he exasperated the High Command, who were normally approached by witnesses of some act of gallantry. Instead, Hughes published colourful accounts of his self-promotion. By the end of summer, the military had had enough of Sam Hughes; they dismissed him from South Africa for military indiscipline and returned him back to Canada. Although Hughes proved to be a competent leader, he was impatient and hugely boastful. He even wrote a letter to the Governor General, Prince Arthur, Duke of Connaught, about his long-time demand for a Victoria Cross and it was of little surprise that the award was refused.

In the First World War he became Minister for Militia and Defence and in 1915, he was knighted. Although he liked to be known as 'Sir Sam', he was still convinced he should have been awarded two VCs, which the War Office were pleased to turn down.

Most of the VCs awarded in the Boer War were for humanitarian actions involving helping wounded comrades to safe places. Another frequent act was riding to the rescue of a fallen comrade whose horse was either killed or had thrown its rider; of the seventy-eight VCs, eighteen involved this last mentioned. One example did not result in a Cross despite involving Britain's greatest wartime prime minister, Winston Churchill. At this time, he was not a politician but a 25-year-old reporter for the *Morning Post* covering the lifting of the siege of Wepener with General Rundle's force.

On 21 April 1900, the 1,400 Imperial Yeomanry, Mounted Infantry and Scouts advanced and found the Boers had seized and held a *kopje*. Under cover, the mounted men waited all day for the 16th Brigade to arrive. In the meantime, men from the Imperial Yeomanry worked their way round the southern flank of the enemy line.

On the 22nd, the Boers saw that the British infantry were not following and delivered a counter-attack that inflicted some casualties on the horsemen. The long-range guns opened fire and the Boer horsemen took refuge behind a rise. Then Angus McNeil, the commander of Montmorency's Scouts, persuaded General Brabazon to let his men cut off their retreat. Some of the fifty scouts called to Churchill to follow them to witness 'a first-class show'. Digging in their spurs, the scouts raced for the *kopje*.

Suddenly, five mounted Boers, along with 200 others, appeared from nowhere. McNeil called a halt and led his men back, accompanied by the Boer's fire. Churchill had dismounted by a wire fence to watch the action. About 120 yards in front of him were half a dozen Boers who opened fire. Churchill wrote in the 22 May edition of the *Morning Post*:

> Then the musketry crashed out, and the 'swish and whirr' of the bullets filled the air. I put my foot in the stirrup. The horse, terrified at the firing, plunged wildly. I tried to spring into the saddle. It turned under the animal's belly. He broke away and galloped madly off.

With no cover to run to, Churchill spotted one of the scouts riding back.

> I shouted to him [Trooper Roberts] as he passed, 'Give me a stirrup.' To my surprise he stopped at once. 'Yes,' he said shortly. I ran up to him, did not bungle the business mounting, and in a moment found myself behind him on the saddle.

Robert's horse was hit and fatally wounded. Churchill recalled he felt the blood on his hand. When they were out of gunshot range, Churchill was effusive in his praise for his rescuer: 'I said, "Never mind, you've saved my life." "Ah," he rejoined, "but it's the horse I'm thinking about."'

Many had witnessed the incident and felt that Roberts deserved the Victoria Cross. Instead, he received the DCM in April 1901. The mane and tail of his mount were taken to England, possibly by Churchill, and returned to Clem Roberts as a woven necklace and a watch cord.

Years later, Roberts wrote to Churchill in an effort to have his DCM elevated to a VC. Churchill replied on 10 December 1913:

> I need not say that I have myself very great admiration for the coolness and courage with which you assisted me at Deetsdorp. I have always felt that unless you had taken me up on your saddle, I should myself certainly been killed or captured, and I spoke myself very strongly to General Rundle on your behalf.
>
> I was very glad to see you have received the Distinguished Conduct Medal [Churchill referred to the medal as the Distinguished Service Medal] – a decoration of very great distinction and honour.

Churchill regretted that with the passage of time and so many brave actions in the Boer War that it was unlikely the War Office would elevate the award. Enclosing a £10 cheque, he went on to end his letter with:

> The DCM is much prized and respected in the Army, and you will no doubt find it a satisfactory memento of what was, beyond all question, a very faithful and self-sacrificing action on your part. Let me, at this distance of time, once again thank you for the service you rendered me.

Another similar case occurred on 27 September 1901, south of Wepener, involving the Sixth New Zealand Contingent, better known as the Mounted Rifles. The patrol marched through the night and camped at 3.00 am about half a mile from Bastard's Drift. Major Andrew sent a nine-man patrol under Corporal Hemphill to the river expecting Commander Du Moulin's men to be on the far bank.

Taken unawares, they ran into some Boers who opened fire at close range. Hemphill's horse was shot dead as the patrol wheeled in retreat. Trooper Ivanhoe Baigent spotted that Hemphill was unhorsed and immediately turned about. Ignoring the heavy fire, he pulled Hemphill up onto his horse and galloped to safety. This ambush held up Major Andrews's advance but later that day they fought off the Boers and secured the drift. Baigent's deed should have merited the Victoria Cross, for which he was recommended. Instead, Baigent received the DCM. In the First World War, he was commissioned and was killed in Palestine.

A case that deserved the Victoria Cross was denied through class distinction and snobbery. George Gill West was born to a retired NCO in the Royal Artillery and, despite his poor background, was an exceptional pupil and was admitted to the Dartmouth Naval College. He was fascinated by science, and skilled at athletics and music. He had a quick grasp of any subject and his exam grades were exceptionally good. There was little doubt that he was in line to become a naval officer. A committee of the College officers, however, decided that West 'lacked a Naval background and financial status which, in his own interest, made commissioned rank impossible to grant'.

Even though he was a still pupil at the Naval College, he left seething with humiliation and anger. He was posted as a deserter, having declared himself 'Absent without Leave'. With the help of his father, who bribed a member of the Union Castle Line to take George to South Africa, he changed his name to John Moore. Arriving in Cape Town, he travelled to Kimberley and found work in the De Beers diamond mines as an electrician, and was the first man to fit an electric light system in a mine. He had a good rapport with the Boers, who allowed him to travel to Cape Town at the outbreak of the war. En route, the train was attacked and he lost all his possessions. Reaching Cape Town, he enlisted in the Cape Town Highlanders and was involved in the Relief of Ladysmith.

On 25 October 1901, George was stationed at the tented Jacobsdaal encampment on the Modder River in the Orange Free State, when the Boers launched a surprise dawn attack. The encampment was by a substantial blockhouse, which was comparatively safe within enemy territory. George had taken cover in the blockhouse when he saw the camp doctor's son try to reach the shelter from outside. The boy was wounded and George made a dash to save him but was repeatedly hit by bullets. He managed to scoop up the boy and carry him to the safety of the blockhouse, where he collapsed. Shortly afterwards, George died of his injuries and was recommended for a posthumous Victoria Cross for his bravery.

A subsequent enquiry found that John Moore was George West, who was still wanted by the Navy for desertion. His VC recommendation was rejected. Instead, he received a posthumous pardon and the DCM.

Another worthy VC recipient was Frank Baxter. A question was raised in Parliament on 21 May 1897 by General John Laurie, Member of Parliament for Pembroke and Haverfordwest:

> I beg to ask the Under Secretary of State for War whether the Secretary of State for War would consider his decision, as announced in a memorandum which appeared in the *London Gazette* of 7th May, with respect to Trooper Frank William Baxter, of the Bulawayo Field Force, in which it is stated that on account of the gallant conduct of this man in having, on 22 April 1896, dismounted and given up his horse to a wounded comrade, Corporal Wiseman, who was being closely pursued by an overwhelming force of the enemy, he would

have been recommended to Her Majesty for the Victoria Cross had he survived; would he recommend to Her Majesty that the Victoria Cross should be conferred on the late trooper on the date of his gallant action, and that the decoration so heroically earned should be forwarded to his nearest relative?

To which Mr William Broderick, the Under-Secretary of State for War, gave the expected reply:

I can assure my Hon. and gallant Friend of the full sympathy of the Secretary of State in his wish to commemorate the noble deed of Trooper Baxter; but the statutes of the Victoria Cross do not contain any provision under which a man who is already dead can be recommended for the distinction. Many cases have occurred in which the Cross would have been awarded had the soldier or sailor survived, but no exception to the rule I have stated has ever been made.

Just before the outbreak of the Anglo-Boer War in 1899, two native uprisings occurred in Rhodesia: the Mashona and Matabele rebellions. It was during the latter that Frank William Baxter of Grey's Scouts performed his life-saving act. Captain Frederick Selous accompanied the expedition and wrote about Baxter's gallantry in his book *Sunshine and Storm in Rhodesia*:

When the scouts were recalled and commenced to retire from the Umguza, after having driven a body of natives from its shelter, as I have already related, they were suddenly fired upon by a party of Matabele who had taken up a position amongst some bush to their left of their line of retreat. They were foremost among the scouts galloped past their ambush, but Capt. Grey with a few in the rear, halted and returned the enemy's fire.

Trooper Wise was the first man hit, and seems to have received his wounds from behind, just as he was mounting his horse, as a bullet struck him high in the back, and travelling up the shoulder-blade, came out near the collar-bone. At this instant, Wise's horse stumbled, and then recovering itself, broke away from its rider, galloping straight back into town, and leaving the wounded man on the ground.

A brave fellow named Baxter at once dismounted and put Wise on his horse, thus saving the latter's life, as it proved, thereby sacrificing his own. Capt. Grey and Lieut. Hook at once went to Baxter's assistance, and they got him along as fast as they could, but the Kaffirs had now closed on them, and were firing out of the bush at very close quarters. Lieut. Hook was shot from behind, the bullet entering the right buttock and coming out near the groin, but most likely, though severing the sciatic nerve, just missing the thigh bone